The Art of Entrepreneurial Outsourcing

100 Mission critical roles you can outsource

By Craig D Robinson

www.craigdrobinson.com

ISBN: **978-1532807909**
Cover Design: Manisha Desgins
Interior Design: Atritex Technologies
Publisher: Blurb Inc.
Editor: Carrie Bean

1. Business 2. Entrepreneurship 3. Management 4.

Outsourcing

Second Edition

Printed in Australia

Contents

The Ethics of Outsourcing

Is it ethical to outsource a job overseas for a significantly reduced cost, rather than employing a local member of your community at a fair market wage?

This is the question repeatedly asked of many business owners. It's a question every business owner should ask themselves before deciding to outsource their mission-critical roles.

The downsides are thrown into the press by unions, pundits and politicians every time a company moves jobs offshore: "Local jobs are lost and our compatriots will suffer as a result of unemployment, and become a burden to the rest of society."

Is that the whole picture?

Aren't there more lives and factors to consider here?

Every time a local job is lost, jobs are created overseas. The reason those countries are able to supply labour so much more cost effectively is because they have a much lower cost of living. They don't enjoy the privileges and opportunities that you and I take for granted.

Isn't providing them meaningful employment an excellent way to support those countries and supplement the foreign aid we send?

It's market-driven, so less likely to be withdrawn on a

whim to fund local election promises. It is supplied efficiently, something government programs notoriously lack. It avoids the corruption rampant in the governments of many developing countries that see large amounts of foreign aid diverted into private bank accounts.

Are those the only benefits?

There is a cost saving to the local business. This means it now has more money to spend on local expansion and resources. It may simply make more profit, pay more in tax and deliver more dividends to its shareholders. The business may lower its prices to become more competitive, leaving local consumers more money to reinvest and spend as they choose. This, in turn, will bring down the cost of living and bring the world one step closer to equality.

Each one of these has a net benefit to the local community.

Is it fair to pay less to an employee because they don't live locally? Let's look at what it costs them to live. For the average worker in a western economy, the essentials of life (food, housing and clothing) take up 63% of the median wage. The remaining 37% is spent on goods that have to be bought at comparatively high local rates.

An offshore worker can pay for food, housing and clothing at significantly reduced rates. The remainder of their income can purchase goods at much lower rates than their western counterparts.

I research the local average salaries for any country I outsource to. I use this to check what I am paying an outsourced worker. I never pay less than double the local median wage for the job they are performing. Imagine if you could get paid double the industry average for your role. What if I told you that you could get paid double to work from home, no more commute in peak hour, so you get to spend more time with your family? You also get to save on travel costs. How does that all sound?

That just leaves the elephant in the room: employee conditions, leave and fair treatment.

By outsourcing, you avoid all the local labour laws and unions, so there is no requirement to look after your workers. No requirement to give them time off and no recourse if you terminate them unfairly.

Fair treatment of offshore employees is left in the hands of business owners. How well has that worked out for the world, historically? After all, unions were formed for a reason.

Thankfully, the world has changed. Social media has made the world a much smaller place. Any employer who mistreats offshore employees risks being exposed by a video on YouTube, losing their customers faster than they can finish watching the clip.

This is far from foolproof, and doesn't affect businesses that operate exclusively to other businesses (B2B).

If you are reading this book, you are considering outsourcing. The decision as to how you treat these offshore employees, whom you will never meet, is up to you. They will cost you 10-15% of what a local employee costs. Are you really going to stint them 1% on paid annual leave?

Basics

You are dealing with people. Your remote staff, those you are outsourcing tasks to, are people. Obvious when you read it, yet surprisingly easy to forget, given you never see them and may not even speak to them. Treat them like people.

People are a pain in the arse. Most of your problems in business come from people. As a manager, it can seem like you spend more time sorting out petty dramas with staff then getting them to do what you pay them for or is it just me? You can't solve this problem by outsourcing.

You may have heard others tell of how outsourcing failed them. You've probably also listened to people who have tried employing people and swear they never will again. Not everyone can manage people effectively, it's hard. Employing staff locally or remotely is not a magic bullet, it's a way to leverage other people's time to get more done, but it has a whole demanding skillset: people management.

With remote staff you won't have office politics, but you still have to manage staff morale and communicate effectively if you want good results. You need to be a good manager to get good results from people. If you aren't a good manager, you can settle for mediocre results, or quit, or you can just learn how to do better.

Keys to getting good results from people:

1. Clarify in your own mind what you want done.
2. Effectively communicate your expectations. Tell them what you want, make sure they understand.
3. Agree on the metrics: how you will measure if they have done a good job, in time to be useful?
4. Offer support during the task; be available to help.
5. Measure: did they achieve the agreed results in time?
6. Reward/sanction.

Too many steps? Try just two – as a senior manager, your life boils down to:

- Reaching agreement.
- Renegotiating agreements.

"Agree" means just that – you tell staff what you want and get them to agree that they can and will do it. Telling them isn't enough, although it's easier and more fun. Ask them how long they need, make sure it is reasonable. Then there is no chance for them to bitch about your unrealistic expectations. This is done behind your back, if you were wondering.

The difficulty you face with remote staff is that they can't just walk to your office and ask what you meant or how you wanted something to look. They only have your written/spoken instructions to go on. So figure out what you want, decide what you need, then record it. Make sure it's clear, concise and readily understood; you will often face language difficulties with remote staff.

The cool bit is that these staff will usually work hard to understand and meet your expectations. They know they are at a disadvantage from the perspective of language and education – they want to overcome that. Plus, you are paying them really well to work from home, compared to what they could earn in their local economy.

If you can figure out steps one and two, you will be able to effectively use remote staff. If your local staff are forever bugging you with stupid questions and producing substandard results, use the same process with them as well!

You are a manager, and you are responsible for the results. The failure of your staff is your failure as a manager. So if you want to get mad at someone when you don't get what you want, find a mirror.

Enough philosophy, let's get down to it...

Define the task

Decide what you want done. Any staff you hire should save you time or solve a problem for your company. What are you trying to achieve?

Outsourcing current tasks

What are you doing at the moment that you don't need to do personally? Are you doing something that...

- o   Is low-level or basic?
- o   Isn't getting you ahead?
- o   You hate?

Got a list – delegate it. All of it. Outsourcing makes this decision easier because it costs you so little.

This is the easiest type of task to outsource, because you are already doing it.

- o   You know what's involved.
- o   You know how long it should take.
- o   You know what the result should look like.

Document what you are doing, how you are doing it and what sort of result you want. Sounds like a drag, right? Why? You are already doing it – so just record that. You've heard the saying, "A picture says a thousand words". So how many does a video say?

Next time you do the task, record it...

On a computer

1. Download a program or app that records your screen.

2. Buy a cheap headset microphone.

Next time you go to do the task you want to outsource, record what you do and explain it as you go. This is simple and effective.

It works even better if you actually grab someone and train them to do it. Have them sit beside you and teach them the task as you go. Every few minutes, pause the recording and ask them if everything makes sense. They will ask you questions like, "How about this?" or "How do you...?" Jot them down, then un-pause the recording.

"You might be wondering how you do this." Repeat their question and provide the answer.

This will appear seamless on the video, and you will have answered the question. This means you will never have to answer the same dumb question again - your staff will simply re-watch the video. They don't want to look dumb asking you a question you've already answered – but they're human, they forget!

Hands-on tasks

1. Buy a go-pro with a head strap.

2. Follow the above steps.

It really helps to have a real person beside you while you are teaching. Things that just seem obvious to you, steps that you don't bother to explain because they are so simple and apparent, will be borderline incomprehensible to them. Your staff member will stop you and ask you to explain the obvious, because they are people and annoying – but do it this once and you'll never have to do it again!

Conceptual tasks

1. Grab your phone's hands-free set or use your Bluetooth headset or car kit.

2. Open a voice recording app.

3. Go to where you can best express yourself: the couch, walking around and gesticulating, driving your car – wherever works for you.

4. Explain the concept.

Act as if you are talking to someone, explaining and teaching. If you need to waffle on – do it. You can always get your remote staff member to summarise it once they have learnt it. A cheap and effective way to boil it down to the most relevant content.

Still need the 'manual'? Have a remote staff member transcribe your video or audio for you.

Outsourcing new and unknown tasks

You don't know what you are doing, but need someone else to effectively do it for you, correct? This is trickier.

How do you clarify and effectively communicate what you need done? You are now only talking about results, not process. It doesn't really matter how they do it, as long as they get results. So, what do you want to achieve? What will happen if this task if completed effectively?

➢ Some are simple. For example, you outsource your SEO and as a result your keywords rank at 1st on Google organic listing.

➢ Some are more difficult. For example, you want an app designed that is cutting edge and utilises trending layouts and functionality, becoming more appealing to younger users.

➢ Some are nearly impossible to measure. For example, you outsource your PR to raise your personal/company profile, as a result you are part of the public consciousness.

Figure out what you want and write it down. Give it to someone to read. Any nuffy will do; you probably have a few working for you. If not, walk outside. The world's full of them. If they can understand what you want to achieve, you're set. They don't need a clue how to do it – after all, you don't know how to do it either! This is a great simplicity test. It makes sure what you want has clarity and almost guarantees understanding. That's why you picked someone a little dim. If it can get through to them, it will likely penetrate any potential language barrier.

The beautiful part of outsourcing like this is that you can't possibly be expected to provide support during the task. You just sit back and wait for results.

Once you have figured out what you want to achieve, have condensed this to a clear and easy-to-understand outline, and passed the idiot test, all you need now is a way to measure the results and the metrics.

Metrics

How do you know when someone has done a good job? Just as importantly, how do they know, before they give it to you and see if you smile or explode. What will empower everyone to decide that the task has been completed on time, effectively and with the desired result? How will you measure success?

Some things are easy to measure, some are hard. Whether through delegated staff tasks or your own goals, you need to know what success looks like. Once you can visualise it, you can find a way to measure it.

If you are paying your remote staff by the hour, you need to set expectations around both results and timeframe. If you are doing this, your measures don't need to be transparent – you measure and if you're not happy, don't hire them again. They have worked the hours, however ineffectively, so they get paid.

If you are paying for results, then the measures need to be more transparent and accessible to both you and your staff.

Some transparent metrics for the examples from the previous pages:

➢ SEO: easy, you are at a particular Google ranking or you aren't.
➢ Functionality of a new app aimed at young users: pick a public forum that is populated by your target

market. Release a beta version, ask them to rate the app in the key areas on a scale of 1-10. If 85% of the testers don't rate it an 8 or higher, the developer doesn't get paid until it is improved.

➢ Raise your profile in the public consciousness: Define what this looks like – more sales, more enquiries, more followers, more website traffic, more Google searches, more mentions by non-partnered people/companies, etc. All of these can easily be measured. Decide what success looks like to you.

Anything can be measured, no matter how intangible. Just delve into it.

If your 10-year goal is to be happy and successful, what does happiness and success look like to you?

Time for family? Set a target: e.g. "in 10 years, I will consistently spend 3 nights a week with my family and one weekend a month away doing activities we choose together."

Financial freedom – how much do you need for that?

Health – "still exercising for 3 hours per week and living without recurring pain in my body."

Anything can be measured. Just figure out what success looks and feels like.

Whilst you can set the metrics, you need agreement from your staff. If they don't think the task, metrics or timeframe are achievable, you have set them up for failure. The easiest way around this is to ask them.

"How would you suggest we measure the results here?" "How long will you need to complete that?"

It is much more powerful when they nominate the metrics and timeframe, leaving fewer excuses for failure.

Support

You need to be available to answer questions and provide support to your staff, not all day, but enough time for any problems that arise to be dealt with swiftly. An effective manager must be accessible.

When managing remote staff, you need to decide the most appropriate ways to communicate. Do you use voice calls, video calls, emails, text message, emailed questions with spoken replies, photos?

Consider:

- o Time zone differences.
- o Language barriers - can they understand you on a call or a recording? *Don't use SMS slang if texting*
- o What works best for you? After all, you are hiring people to make your life easier!

Once you have established what will work, establish timeframes. If they are on the other side of the world, it's easy as you have all day to answer last night's questions. If you are offset by only half a day, you may need to be more specific and disciplined with your response time. If they work from 2pm to 10pm your time, you may agree to answer questions at 5.30pm each evening to allow them to maximise output for the second half of their day, then again before 2pm the next day – answers ready for them to start that day's work.

Trust, but verify

Regular communication is also essential for you to know what your staff are doing. Are they on track? Are they likely to meet your expectations?

In the early days the question of "Have I hired a scammer?" may arise. There are people who will try and bill 6 employers for their time each hour. Many outsourcing platforms have a provision for you to view what work is being done, such as a screen-shot at random times during each hour. You can also have your staff download a work-tracking program. *For information on the best and latest programs and platforms, visit* www.CraigDRobinson.com

This still won't rule out a smart scammer. A daily update will help assess how staff are progressing. Just a brief summary of what they spent their time on and how the sub-task is progressing. This can work really well with under-performing local staff as well. It makes people accountable for their time. When they realise you will see that they put 2 hours next to a simple task, they will be inclined to stop procrastinating get things done.

For larger projects, incorporating key milestones allows you to:

- o Ensure the timeframe is adhered to.
- o Assess progress and effectiveness.
- o Guide faltering or wandering projects back onto the track you envisaged.

Reward/Sanction

Let your staff know when you are happy with their work. Take action when they are not performing.

That is all.

But seriously, it's lonely working solo even from home. There is no body language or office gossip to fill the feedback gap – so make sure you let them know how you feel they are doing.

Be realistic with your expectations. They are people who don't have your education, quality of life or opportunities. You are helping to change that by employing them at a wage significantly above what they can earn locally. You are often supporting a whole family through their income.

Also be realistic. If it's not working and they are not improving fast enough, move on. You are providing opportunity, not charity.

Just make sure you tell them what you're feeling about their work.

Recruitment

Clarify what you want

Look at your task and be sure you know what you need done. Can you...

- o Accurately describe it to a stranger?
- o Clearly articulate your expectations?
- o Describe how you will measure success?

If you can, you are ready to delegate out this task.

Required skillset

What skills will your remote staff member need? Make a list of everything you can think of. Now, sort this list into:

- o Must Have.
- o Should Have.
- o Could Have.

Now write an assessment to test for these traits in potential remote staff.

If you need someone to transcribe your handwritten meeting notes and voice recordings, attach samples of both with the job posting. If the task is more in-depth, ask for examples of previous work and have 10 questions they need to answer about it, things that show understanding of the concepts. Throw in red herrings.

Have a second round of assessments ready for

shortlisted candidates to make sure they didn't just look up or outsource their answers. Send them these with a time limit.

Some outsourcing platforms have tests that staff can do and post with their profiles. You can sort results based on how they performed. There are a number of online work assessment businesses that you can use to assess staff skills (www.CraigDRobinson.com *for more info).*

Post the ad

Decide if you are going to pay on results or by the hour.

Paying by results, or value-based billing, is lower risk – everyone knows what they are getting, when and for how much. It has some pitfalls:

- o You must be very specific and clear about what you want. You will get what you ask for and only that. If you didn't provide sufficient clarity around your expectations, you will be disappointed.
- o It can be expensive to change the scope of a project part-way through. They have done part of the work – you have to pay what they ask for the expanded scope, or get someone else to start from scratch.

Paying by the hour can be a great way to get ripped off. It can also be a great way to allow you to collaborate with some remarkable people, and utilise their talent and ability to develop results far beyond what you originally proposed.

Tips when hiring on hourly rate:

- o   If possible, hire for a couple of small, fixed-price projects first. This lets you test competency and ensures they are not just con-artists.
- o   Use a work-tracking program or work-view function within the outsourcing program in the early days. Once trust is established, this becomes less essential.
- o   Get daily work summaries – read them and give feedback, everyday initially, then at random and unpredictable intervals.
- o   Hammer the communication.

Create Selection Criteria

What level do they need to score on each assessment for their application to progress?

Look at their previous work history. Have they completed many previous tasks? What was their feedback score? I will usually sort candidates on feedback score, then look at their pricing or hourly rate.

Have they got relevant previous experience? If you are outsourcing a job that you can't do yourself, then their knowledge and experience needs to be established through previous successful projects.

How much are you willing to spend?

Give them a score based on how you feel about their:

- o Clarity and professionalism.
- o Timeliness.
- o Effective communication.
- o Overall fit and 'gut feeling'.

Make sure they have an internet connection of sufficient speed, capacity and reliability to download and handle the work.

Hire them on a trial basis, and have objective assessment criteria set in place first to monitor their initial work and improvements in their output.

Interview like Any Other Candidate

You are hiring a staff member, so put them through your usual interview process.

Ask for references – not just an email address, but the name of the person and business they worked for. Google the business and contact them through your own channels.

Consider candidate profiling – DiSC, Myers-Briggs or other psychometric profiling.

Maximise your efficiency and get the most out of your limited time. Wherever possible, I like to use the NET concept – No Extra Time.

How can I achieve more in my day without spending any extra time working?

There are a number of ways you can do this.

Any time you are training a new staff member, record it. If it is computer-based training, use a program to record the screen and a microphone to record your voice. Every few minutes, pause the recording, ask if they have any questions. Note the questions, turn the recording back on and say,

"You might be wondering how you do this". Repeat their question and provide the answer.

You now have a training video that will save you time when you hire for that role again. You can have it polished and edited by a remote video and audio editor. If you want, they can produce it as a professional training video at low cost. You can also have it transcribed as the basis for your written operations manual.

If you are completing a task you want systemised, put your phone's hands-free headset on and start your voice recording app. Talk through what you are doing and record it, then get it transcribed. You now have a standard operation procedure for that process.

It doesn't take you any extra time to talk through your actions whilst you complete them.

When you are driving, do the same thing – record your thoughts on a topic and have them transcribed. You now have an article you can post, an email you can send, minutes of that meeting you just left or notes from that call with a client.

You can get an app that will automatically upload your recordings to your cloud storage. Hire a remote staff member who can understand and interpret your voice in a noisy environment. Have them check the cloud storage daily, transcribe your voice notes and email them to you.

I like to take handwritten notes during meetings. Afterwards I usually want to send the client an email to confirm what we discussed. I photograph these notes on my phone, again, with an app that automatically uploads to the cloud when I hit a Wi-Fi zone. My Virtual Assistant types these and saves them in the client's folder on the cloud.

I now have a record of the meeting, and can copy and paste the sections I want to confirm via email.

Be creative; what other tasks are you doing that you could use the NET principle with?

Using This Book

Each topic is broken into 4 parts:

Results

The tangible result you will achieve with this concept.

Summary

A description of the concept to give you ideas on how you might implement it. If you are pushed for time, or it just makes sense, you can skip this part entirely.

Selection Criteria

The qualities you should be looking for in a remote staff member for this task and the indicators you can use to identify those.

Some topics also have a subsection entitled Assessments.

These are tests you might use to further establish the suitability of the staff member.

Metrics

These are the measures you should establish before hiring. The remote staff member can use these to measure success. You can use them to decide whether to release payment or accept the work.

Admin and Assistant Duties

1. Transcription Notes

Result

Have a digital copy of your hand-written notes from meetings or seminars.

Summary

It is acceptable to take notes by hand during a meeting with a client or colleague, whilst it can be seen as rude to do so on a tablet or device. You don't seem to be paying attention to the other person when using a tablet or computer, as you could be checking your emails or doing many things not related to the assigned task.

The problem with handwritten notes is that they are difficult to track and file, and easy to lose. And we all know that transcribing those meeting or seminar notes onto your computer is just a drag!

To solve these problems, download a photo app to your phone that will automatically sync to your cloud storage. Once the meeting is over, photograph the handwritten pages. Once you are in Wi-Fi range, the phone will automatically upload them to the cloud.

You then ask your remote staff member to transcribe these for you and send you the completed file. If they are your regular or full-time assistant, you may even have them file the notes directly to the appropriate directory on the cloud.

If you write the file name at the top of the page, the staff member will know what to call the file. Make sure you number the pages, ie page 1 of 6, so they know how many pages to look for. Photos will be uploaded separately, one for each page.

Selection Criteria

- o Ability to touch-type effectively.
- o Ability to understand your handwriting.

Assessment

- o Attach a sample page of your handwriting and have them transcribe it as part of their job application.
- o Have them take a WPM touch typing test.

Metrics

- o Error-free copy returned to you. Agree on an acceptable error rate, say 2 errors per 500 words, depending on how legible or otherwise your handwriting is.
- o Completed in agreed timeframe or simply agree an amount per 100 words.
- o Correctly filed in the appropriate directory on your cloud server.

2. *Dictation or Meeting Minutes*

Result

Have your spoken notes or minutes of a meeting transcribed.

Summary

This is a great way to make 'dead' time more productive. When you leave a meeting, put on your hands-free headphones or car hands-free kit. Record your notes on a voice memo app on your phone, and then have them transcribed and emailed to you.

You can download an app that will record voice memos and upload directly to the cloud.

You can place your phone in the middle of a table during a meeting to record the proceedings, then upload the file and receive a full transcript of the meeting. This will give you a full record of what was said and can be used to create the minutes in order to save you frantically scribbling notes during the meeting and not fully taking part.

This is also a great way to record your ideas, articles or blog posts. When you are 'stuck' and find yourself staring at a blank screen, go for a walk or drive. Move around and get your blood flowing. Put your hands-free headset on and just talk. You can always edit the content later, or have that done for you.

You can also use this method to create policy or training documents. Record yourself as you teach a new staff member, then get it transcribed so you have a permanent training document.

This is a great time saver and allows you to use the principle of No Extra Time to get more done.

Selection Criteria

- o Must be able to understand your spoken words in a noisy environment and transcribe accurately.

Assessment

- o Upload a sample recording and have it transcribed.

Metrics

- o Error-free copy returned to you. As before, agree on an acceptable error rate, say 2 errors per 500 words, depending on how legible your handwriting is.
- o Completed in agreed timeframe, or simply agree an amount per 100 words.
- o Correctly filed in the appropriate directory on your cloud server.

3. *Travel Arrangements*

Result

Get your plane tickets sorted, rental car or accommodation booked, all for the best available price and all without wasting half a day.

Summary

It can be frustrating to have to compare different flights, car rentals, hotels and holiday deals. Why not have someone do the research for you?

Define what you are looking for. Do you have a set destination or are you looking for a cost-effective holiday? Does it matter what time you fly? What style of accommodation are you happy with? What style of rental car or transfer?

Once you have set the parameters, get them to come back to you with options and prices. You may want them to provide you with links to the various options so you can inspect the websites yourself.

If you have an ongoing relationship with your staff member, you may have them make the bookings for you.

I have a separate bank account with a debit MasterCard linked to it. This allows online purchases to be made but does not allow the account to be overdrawn. It is linked to my internet banking and I only transfer small amounts of money in at any given time.

Using safeguards like this, you can even provide remote staff with a card number to pay for purchases whilst minimising your risk of fraud.

Selection Criteria

- o Ability to understand and follow directions.
- o History of research tasks.
- o Rely heavily on the feedback from previous clients: Have they done this sort of work before? Did they do it well?

Metrics

- o The arrangements meet your criteria.
- o The price matches your budget and is the best available price. Pick one aspect of the travel arrangements and spend 15 minutes checking to see if you can find a better price for the same or comparable services.

4. Calendar and Appointment Management

Result

Manage your time and diary to allow you to get more work done and appear more professional.

Summary

People who are really good at what they do are in high demand. They are busy and booked up. The fact that people need to schedule a meeting or phone call with you, and that they have to go through a staff member to do so, indicates that you are busy and successful.

You can save time shooting emails or messages backwards and forwards trying to fix a time with another busy person. You have someone to follow-up and confirm the day before to ensure you don't waste time traveling to a meeting someone has forgotten.

Scheduling meetings lets you focus on what you are doing without distraction. People will be impressed by your structure and learn there is no point calling you to discuss something or requesting a meeting directly with you. You will refer them to your remote staff member. More time is freed up!

You will need to have a cloud-based calendar, but I'd recommend you do this anyway. This lets you access your appointments from all your devices, usually offline as well.

Selection Criteria

- o Understanding of the diary or cloud calendar software you use.
- o Ability to write professionally.
- o Ability to speak professionally.
- o Able to work your standard working hours; aim for a similar time zone to your own.
- o Internet connection speed that allows them to make clear voice calls.

Metrics

- o All meeting requests during business hours responded to within 2 hours.
- o All meetings and calls confirmed the business day prior.
- o All meetings you have to attend are organised to minimise travel.
- o Diary organised to maximise your working time and minimise interruptions.

5. *Email Management*

Result

A cleaner inbox, with emails prioritised and sorted for you. Replies drafted for your approval.

Summary

We all know what it is like to have a busy day and come back to a packed inbox. Emails are taking up more and more time for companies. In 2015, this is estimated at 28% of standard working time for an average employee!

Give a remote staff member your email login details. Let them sift and sort your emails for you, prioritise, organise and draft replies.

If you use cloud-based email, this is simple, as they will organise it for you and then you will see what they see. If your emails are handled by software on your computer, have your email manager send you a summary email with the priorities listed. Also, arrange for a 'drafted reply' email with all the drafts ready to be cut and pasted into each email by you.

If you are able to engage a full-time or ongoing Virtual Assistant, you can formulate a priority contact list, so they understand who is important in your world, and whose emails can be safely relegated further down the list.

It can be a good idea to set up a second email account that only your email manager has access to. Set this account up on your phone and make sure it is the only account that is set with an audible alert. If something urgent arrives in your inbox, your email manager can notify you straight away to your private email, that way you can get to it immediately.

Having the replies drafted for you saves the bulk of the tedious work in replying. Often, all the sender wants is to have their email acknowledged.

Selection Criteria

- o Understands professional email writing protocol.
- o Ability to read and write your language to a high level.
- o Able to work the same hours as your standard work day. A time zone +/- 4 hours usually allows this.

Metrics

- o Your emails are prioritised for you in the timeframe set, e.g. hourly.
- o You get notified of urgent emails from selected contacts.
- o Replies are drafted in a professional manner

6. *Data Entry*

Result

Have large amounts of data accurately entered into a workable, digital format.

Summary

Data entry has got to be about the worst job for someone with an active mind. Copying large amounts of written material – there is a reason that teachers set this as punishment in school!

This is an obvious task to outsource. The problem you face is ensuring that the job is done accurately, as anyone is going to get bored doing it.

If you physically have the data, you need to get it to your virtual staff member first. If it is on consistently sized paper, a photocopier/scanner with an automatic document feeder can scan this onto a memory stick for you quickly and effectively.

If that's not an option, use the camera on your phone. It is high resolution and can take photos quickly. Download an app that lets you take photos and send straight to a cloud storage device. With the phone in one hand, you can flip over each page with the other hand to photograph a large number of documents quickly. It may be worth dialling down the picture capture quality on your phone so you don't blow your data allowance.

Selection Criteria

- o Ability to read the language you are using.
- o Touch typing ability, including the number keypad on the keyboard.

Assessment

- o Have them enter 2-3 pages of sample data. Upload this with the job so they know you aren't just getting work done for free; every applicant will data enter the same pages, so you don't really have a big win.

Metrics

- o Have a set rate for each amount of data entered, e.g. per page.
- o Have half the agreed rate as 'retainer' and the other half paid only if data is free from sufficient errors, i.e. less than 1 error per 5 pages.
- o Make sure you highlight any errors and send back to your remote staff member to verify so they know you aren't just ripping them off.

7.   Call Answering and Screening

Result

Appear more important by having a personal assistant who answers and screens all your calls, a 'gatekeeper'.

Stop the distraction of your phone ringing all the time.

Summary

Having someone who answers your phone calls signals success. It shows your time is valuable and not to be taken for granted.

If you have a Voiceover IP system set up, diverting your phone is easy and calls can easily be transferred back.

Even if you are using traditional mobiles or landlines, it is still achievable. Divert your phone to a local internet number that you set up. This will transfer your call to your remote staff member without horrendous cost, as you will pay any call forwarding charges. Your remote staff member will answer calls on your behalf.

If it is not an urgent call, or if you are busy, the staff member can take a message and pass that on to you at a convenient time. If it is urgent, they can page you and transfer the call back. Most modern phones will let you selectively forward calls, or have a 'private mode' that forwards all calls but those from a selected group of numbers, e.g. your assistants.

If you can't do this, a second phone is required. It can be a landline with a private number or a second mobile.

This can be a roundabout way of getting calls, so investigate VOIP. It's cheaper anyway.

Establish a list of priority contacts, so your remote staff member knows who to put through and who to delay. Also, give them read-only access to your diary so they know when not to disturb you.

Selection Criteria

- o Ability to speak your language fluently
- o Ability to understand a wide range of voice types and accents in your language; they will get calls from a wide range of people.

Assessment

- o Conduct a phone screen with them.
- o Have 4 staff members or friends call them and test them.
- o Make the calls from noisy environments.

Metrics

- o Calls are quickly answered and assessed; have a colleague call randomly to check quality.
- o Messages are succinct and accurately passed on
- o Professional in all their dealings

8. *Event Planning*

Result

Organise and coordinate many different people and contractors to have an event run seamlessly.

Summary

Anyone who has ever organised an event knows what a nightmare it can be. Heck, there is an entire industry devoted to it!

Communicating with all the people involved, getting feedback on when they are available and what they are required for, it all takes time.

Sketch out your basic requirements, get the remote staff member to research options for various functions and contracts. Have them provide you with a list, including a summary of options, costs, availability and links to online content about each.

Make your selection and have the staff member contact each person/company to confirm acceptance of their offer and explain requirements. Any clarifying questions can have answers drafted by the staff member before being approved by you.

Set up an internet call number. This is a local phone number that diverts to the offshore location of your staff member via the internet. They can take messages and answer basic questions. Too often, people just need handholding or are just too lazy to organise their thoughts into an email, so they call and waste your time. This resolves that.

Selection Criteria

- o Ability to communicate effectively and professionally in your language, both written and spoken.
- o Should be able to work your normal working hours; a time zone +/- 4 hours should allow this.
- o Ability to plan and coordinate – check their work history.
- o You may even want a formal qualification in event management.

Assessment

- o Conduct a phone interview to assess their language skills.
- o Have them draft a sample letter of offer.

Metrics

- o Promptly provide responses to your questions.
- o Provide clear daily summaries on who they have contacted and why.
- o Provide timetables, prices and contact lists for all parties involved.

9. *Fact Checking*

Result

Have credible references for facts and figures you quote.

Summary

Did you know that 72% of all statistics are made up on the spot?

Most people are a bit wary of facts and numbers they get without supporting evidence. You either have to say "Trust me," or, "I read it somewhere..." Neither is believable.

Having credible references for any facts you provide in a professional setting makes you appear more reliable and shows you are thorough in your work and preparation.

Any time you are using facts in your work, highlight them in the document and send them to your remote admin assistant to verify. They can find credible references for the fact and then reference the fact to a footnote.

If the document is going to be sent digitally, simply insert the fact as a hyperlink that takes the reader directly to the online reference library.

Selection Criteria

- o   Ability to research effectively.
- o   A bachelor's degree will usually indicate the staff

member understands what a credible reference is and how to correctly reference it within a business document.

Assessment

- o Attach a sample document with 3-5 facts highlighted and have them provide references for the facts.

Metrics

- o References are credible to the standard you require; any reference to "statistics for dummies.com" may have a detrimental effect on your credibility.
- o References are relevant and appropriate to the fact.

Result

Have your online file structure ordered, logical and referenced.

Summary

When you work on so many different documents, it can be difficult to have them always in a logical and systematic order where anyone can find them. It usually makes sense to the person who filed it, but once the information needs to be accessed by a greater number of people, problems can occur.

Having someone spend time categorising, filing and referencing every document you have ever created can be a big job. Until now, the cost of this time meant it was only embarked upon when it became essential. With outsourcing and cloud storage, it has become accessible to all.

Start by making a local backup of all your files!

Give your remote staff member access to your cloud storage. Have them go into each file and assess its contents. Get them to document the title, subject, author (if known), last revision date, any keywords, and the file location. Have all this placed in a database that can be easily searched.

Once all documents have been assessed, have the staff member suggest a draft file tree. You can assess and approve this first. Once you are happy, they can move each file to the appropriate directory. Don't worry, you can always search the database to find where they have been moved to!

Selection Criteria

- o Ability to use the software you typically use to create documents.
- o Ability to read and comprehend complex documents relating to your business.
- o Ability to create and manage a database.

Assessment

- o Provide 3-5 documents and have them provide the subject, keywords, and a two-sentence summary for each.

Metrics

- o Database is a true representation of the files catalogued.
- o All information on the database is accurate, especially the file locations listed.
- o File tree is logical, ordered and files are placed where agreed.

11. Letter Writing

Result

Have letters professionally drafted and personalised to the individual.

Summary

You will need to give your remote staff member the gist of what you want each letter to say. This can be done effectively by voice recording.

You can dictate the general letter and have them put it into a professional format. This is especially useful for those who struggle with etiquette when dealing with and writing to difficult individuals.

If you want to contact clients, you can give your staff member access to your Customer Relationship Management system, or CRM. This way they can add personal touches to each letter so the client doesn't feel they are just part of a mass campaign or mail merge.

If you want to contact someone you haven't contacted before, ask the staff member to research this person so the recipient feels they are receiving personal correspondence drafted specifically for them.

This is an effective way to overcome the 'spam' mentality that many people take when they get a letter about something they haven't asked for.

Selection Criteria

- o Ability to write creatively and well.
- o Understanding of professional letter-writing etiquette.
- o Ability to understand your dictation.
- o Able to research content.

Assessment

- o Provide a dictation of a letter, just stating the general outline. Have this converted into a professional letter as part of the application.

Metrics

- o Correspondence is grammatical, correctly structured and reads well.
- o Any personal touches added match the individual to whom the letter is addressed.

12. Grant Writing

Result

Have a polished and bespoke grant application completed, without wasting days of your life.

Summary

Completing a grant application is an onerous process. It can chew up hours or days in taking the knowledge you have and laying it out in the format required.

Chances are that if you have done this before, you are keen to avoid repeating this experience. If you have completed grant applications before, you have also laid out most of the salient information.

If you are able to pull together old grant applications, as well as giving a remote staff member access to as much data on yourself or your organisation as possible, they will be well on their way to reformatting the information in a unique way for the grant application.

Once you have the grant application, send it straight on to the staff member. Let them assess it, see what they think they can complete and what they think they will need more information on.

Have them send you a bullet-point list of questions and requests for information. You can either write replies or simply dictate your responses.

By passing on the information, rather than answering the specific questions yourself, you empower the staff member to answer all the questions.

You also save yourself time and avoid the common staff issue of having all the tough questions thrown at you to handle. If they know they will end up answering them anyway, they are more likely to give it a go.

Selection Criteria

- o Ability to write in a professional and engaging way.
- o Ability to research and compile information.

Assessment

- o A written assessment on a topic you nominate.
- o Consider a professional test on 'abstract reasoning'. This tests the ability to draw accurate conclusions from limited information.

Metrics

- o Thorough, complete and professional grant application completed.

  If you are unhappy with a section, send it back with notes until it is completed.

13. Policy and Procedure Writing

Result

Have a complete and detailed Operations Manual for your business.

Summary

Accumulated knowledge is one of the most valuable resources you gain from trained staff. Over time, they have learned the best way to do things. They have experimented and modified procedures to find a way to get the best, or at least an acceptable, result with the least amount of effort.

What we want is to capture and replicate this knowledge, in order to streamline the business and get consistent results.

This not only sets the standard to which work should be completed, it also makes training of new staff much simpler and less costly. Recording that accumulated knowledge is also insurance for when you lose a staff member – you haven't lost all their learned knowledge.

The writing of an Operations Manual takes time, though.

This is another great time to use No Extra Time principles. You could either ask the staff member to record their screen, or you could video their activities. It is most beneficial to have them explain to someone who is physically with them whilst they do this.

Of course, the best time to do this is when you do actually hire and train a new staff member. This is a golden opportunity to capture the training data.

Then you just upload the video and audio to your remote staff member and have them transcribe it. You may even choose to have them create a script for a polished and professional training video instead of a massive paper manual.

Selection Criteria

- o Ability to understand and transcribe the spoken recordings of yourself and your staff.
- o Ability to understand the concept of your work is a big advantage. Look for someone with formal qualifications in your area of business.

Assessment

- o Post a short video and audio file and have it submitted as a finished product.

Metrics

- o Clear, accurate and well summarised information returned.
- o Difficult to negotiate a set figure, so use a time-tracking software and ensure you are getting your money's worth.

14. Ordering of Tailor-made Clothes

Result

Get a personally tailored, up-to-date and extensive wardrobe incredibly cheaply.

Summary

If you haven't visited South-east Asia and had suits and clothes tailor-made at prices you couldn't purchase the fabric for back home, you probably know someone who has.

The issue is usually that you need to travel to the country to get the clothes made. If you aren't planning a holiday, then a specific trip eliminates the cost savings.

Utilising a remote staff member in a SE Asian country, you can eliminate this problem.

Download a clothing measurement chart from the internet. Have a friend who has made clothes before take your measurements, or pay a local tailor to measure you.

Pick clothes you want, either from photos on the internet, or by visiting local boutiques and using your phone's camera to capture pictures of what you like.

Send all this info to your remote staff member. Have them find a local tailor and negotiate on price. They can photograph fabric swatches and send them to you for approval.

Start with a small order and be prepared to post it back with notes on what you want altered. Alternatively, you can send over some old clothes that fit you well and have the tailor use those to copy size, although they will probably also just copy the cut as well.

Once established, you can have a regular stream of current-season clothes, tailor-made to your specifications. Every item an original!

NOTE: Be aware that in South East Asia, most fabric is light weight. This is key if you live in a cold climate.

Selection Criteria

- o Lives in a SE Asian country.
- o Has a postal address you can ship parcels to.
- o Able to communicate effectively with you.
- o Someone who cares about what they wear and how they look.

Metrics

- o Clothes delivered within budget and on time.
- o Once sizing and style have been established, you want consistent fit for your garments.

15. Gift Shopping

Result

Get the perfect gift for every occasion without having to spend hours shopping.

Summary

Gift shopping can be painful and time-consuming. With the proliferation of online shopping, this is a perfect task to outsource.

Define who you are shopping for and your budget. If you have established trust with the remote staff member, give them your Facebook login details, as this will let them more accurately assess the interests, recent activities and likes of the person they are shopping for.

I have a separate bank account with a debit MasterCard linked to it. This allows online purchases to be made but does not allow the account to be overdrawn. It is linked to my internet banking and I only transfer small amounts of money in at a time.

Using safeguards like this, you can minimise your risk of fraud. Alternatively, you could set up a separate PayPal account with just this card linked to it. That way you can simply change passwords if you have to change staff members.

Have the gifts sent to your home for wrapping. Unless it's

for your wife.

Some online shopping businesses will even offer gift wrapping and card writing, with you providing the content. This way you can send a personal gift to someone who isn't having a party.

This enables you to show you care with the least amount of stress and effort possible. After all, it's the thought that counts.

Selection Criteria

o   You are going to have to trust this person's judgement, so you need to like them first. Once you have a shortlist of applicants, do several voice interviews to ensure you get along.

o   Pick someone whose taste you like. Ask to be added to their Facebook and check their photos, pages they like and their interests.

o   Although it may cost a little more, it is probably best to go with someone who lives in a similar country and socio-economic environment. They will understand the culture better.

Metrics

o   Gifts are selected for your approval on time and within budget.

o   Gifts arrive at their destination when they are supposed to.

Research and Data Collection

16. Build a Database of Potential Clients

Result

Have a database of potential clients within your target demographic whom you can market to.

Summary

Marketing is a lot more effective when you can target the customers you want as they will be more likely to buy from you.

The first thing you need is clarity around what those customers look like. How old are they? Where do they live? Are you targeting a specific gender? How much do they earn? What type of job and level of education do they have?

Create an 'avatar' of your perfect customer. Now you are ready to start building your database.

Task your remote staff member to find the names and contact details of a specific number of potential customers or clients.

If you are a B2B business, this will be a lot easier, as businesses usually advertise. If you want people in a specific role within the business, a LinkedIn search will usually show this up. A premium LinkedIn subscription will get you their contact details. Alternatively, you can guess it. There are only a few different email protocols, joe.smith@, j.smith@, JoeS@, etc. Try them all until you find a winner.

If you are a B2C business, it can be a bit harder. However social media has made your life considerably easier. Once your remote staff member identifies a customer that matches your criteria, they can use a number of online tools to find contact details for them.

Those who meet the criteria, add them to your database.

Warning: Make sure you understand your local electronic marketing and unsolicited mail laws.

Selection Criteria

- o   Ability to think creatively to find information.
- o   Excellent online ability.

Assessment

- o   Check how easy it is to find your contact details online, e.g. Google your own email address. Require all applicants to find your contact details using the limited information you provide and email through their applications.

Metrics

- o   Achieve a set number of names on the database.
- o   Trust but verify: randomly verify a set number of contacts to ensure they are real.

17. Staff Newsletter

Result

Produce a consistent, engaging newsletter to keep all staff updated about events in the company.

Summary

Ever tried a staff newsletter? It's good for morale, great for vertical communication and goals alignment at all levels. But it's a damned pain in the arse to produce, unless you have the spare cash to throw the job at a Personal Assistant.

For the rest of us, we need an alternative, or we'll have to work longer hours.

Outsourcing this role to a creative writer makes great sense. Send them to your company website as a start, so they get a feel for what you do.

Each month, have them submit 5-10 articles they have researched on areas they feel are relevant to your business. You review these and pick the 2-3 that are truly relevant and have them summarised by the remote writer for inclusion.

Have the writer do a 10-15 minute interview with a high-performing staff member to get some tips on a particular area. Have them write up these tips as an article then send it to the staff member to review and provide feedback.

Do a 'staff-member-in-profile' article using the same voice interview technique. This piece is a get-to-know-someone article, great to bring a team closer as everyone gets to learn others' interests and passions.

Of course, you need the 'Director's Desk' or similar, but I think you know the format now.

With just a few minutes on the phone and reviewing a few articles, you have produced a low-cost staff newsletter.

Selection Criteria

- o Creative writing ability – view previous work.
- o Ability to converse easily and your language.
- o Ability to interview.
- o Negotiate a set monthly fee for the newsletter.

Assessment

- o Have shortlisted candidates conduct an interview with a staff member and write an article.

Metrics

- o Articles submitted for review each month on time and with relevant content.
- o Interviews are done as scheduled.
- o Articles are engaging and relevant.
- o Layout is pleasing and professional.

18. Competitor Research

Result

Find out what your competition is doing, their key selling points and sales pitch.

Summary

Knowing what your competitors do and how they do it, especially the most successful ones, is the first step in matching and beating them.

Any good business plan should include 'Competition Analysis' as a key component.

To find out what your competitors are doing, brief a remote staff member on who your ideal client is. Have them pose as your ideal client to your competition and enquire about a directly competing product.

Remember, you want to know how they handle a client that you want for your own, buying something that you want to sell them.

Get the staff member to record all aspects of the interaction, follow-up, sales process and pitch.

Selection Criteria

○   Ability to pose effectively as a potential customer. This will entail different skills, depending on your industry. Do they need in-depth technical knowledge or just the ability to speak your language?

Assessment

- o Have them try posing as a client to one of your local staff members.

Metrics

- o Accurate and detailed information that matches what you already know and understand about your competitor.

19. Market Research

Result

Find out what your customers want and if there is a market for a proposed product or service.

Summary

Conducting market research prior to launching any new product or service, or entering a new market, is sound practice which every business should follow.

Define the purpose of your market research, the key information you want to obtain from this research, and the ins and outs and the scope of research you want undertaken.

Define the target customer, their geographic location, age group or gender, any and all other specifics.

In case you have conducted any internal survey or prepared a questionnaire, share these with your chosen researchers.

Some companies will provide you with a client list, but be wary here: trust but verify that they are real names. Alternatively, you can create your own. (See Client Database creation).

Specifically communicate the timeframe within which the research should be completed, and the form and manner in which the report should be presented in order to enable the easiest interpretation of the findings.

Selection Criteria

o Know the size of agency in terms of manpower and revenue, and how long have they been in the research industry.

o Look out for people who you feel can gel with your team and learn about their data collection techniques. Opt for someone who collects timely data and covers a minimum of 30 rounds of interviews to collect meaningful data.

o Opt for someone who agrees on deliverables, provides a clear statement of work with clear agenda and timeframes/milestones.

o Ask for their successful client list, and look at the type of businesses they have handled.

Metrics

o Research results which enhance your knowledge about your own business and its market.

o Provides tremendously useful data at reasonable cost.

o Verifiable results – do random checks and call-backs with potential customers who were contacted.

20. Procurement

Result

Get a price and feature breakdown, and comparison on any large transaction your company is going to enter into.

Summary

Shopping around will get you the best price, but it is time-consuming. When you are paying the salary of a local staff member to shop around and compare the prices and features of various goods and services, the cost saving can quickly be eaten up with the cost of their time.

Tasking a remote staff member to it is a far more effective way to get a detailed comparison and breakdown.

It doesn't matter whether it's a new phone company for your staff phones, office furniture, earth-moving equipment or project management services.

If you can define what you need and explain it to someone, you can task a remote staff member to find prices.

Remember, the more specific you are, the better the results will be. Set the requirements as tightly as you can, including location, timeframe, quality required, etc.

You can have as much information provided as you like,

or if you prefer, just names and prices.

Selection Criteria

- o Effective written and spoken communication.
- o Ability to work during your business hours, geographically aligned with your longitude as closely as possible.
- o Ability to use a spreadsheet or database software compatible with that used in your office.

Assessment

- o Have candidates research an area you have already looked into extensively. See who gets as many options as you found.

Metrics

- o Thorough, detailed and well-presented comparison table.
- o All options match your criteria.
- o Completed within set timeframe.

21. Topical and Individual Research

Result

Have thorough, in-depth research conducted into any topic. Provide relevant information referenced back to credible sources.

Summary

Whether you are looking at launching a new line, researching a potential staff member, or looking to nail a sales presentation, good information helps you make good decisions.

Having someone spend the time to research the topic you are looking at, locating the most relevant and credible information saves you time and money.

A competent researcher will be able to provide you with an executive summary of the information to save you reading all the articles. You can peruse the exec summary and isolate the most appropriate data and only read that in-depth.

A researcher with a strong skillset in social media can find out phenomenal information about individuals. Whether it is a potential staff member or potential client, information is power. The right background information can allow you to make the right key hiring decision, or fine-tune that sales pitch to land you the deal.

Remember, the more details you can provide upfront, the better your backend result will be.

Selection Criteria

- o Ability to think creatively to find information.
- o Excellent online ability.

Assessment

- o Consider a professional test on 'abstract reasoning'. This tests the ability to draw accurate conclusions from limited information.
- o Have them research you, see what information they come back with (good to know, anyway).

Metrics

- o Detailed and relevant information presented in a well-organised and easily-understood fashion.
- o Have links to original data source for verification.
- o Conduct random audits to see if you or an independent expert can locate more information. Make sure the check is done only using the same information.

Human Resources and Local Staff Management

22. Payroll Processing

Result

Have your payroll completed and submitted for you to process.

Summary

Ensuring all your staff are correctly paid each pay-cycle is a time-consuming job, yet a crucial one with many factors to consider.

Have you factored in allowances, that travel you asked them to do, reimbursement of costs, overtime, leave loadings, sick pay management and verification? The list goes on.

If you use a cloud-based payroll system, this is a piece of cake. If you use local software, you can usually get a copy to your remote staff member to use. If it is common software, outsource to someone who already has a licenced copy.

Send them all relevant information. Ideally, have your staff send details to a specific email address. Give your remote staff member access to this email address so they can receive and enter all data.

You will need to set rules around it. For example, if there is medical certificate received, does it go to you to verify? Which manager signs off travel and expenditure?

Have the staff member send you a spreadsheet showing issues and irregularities with the pay run for you to review, prior to processing the salary payments.

Selection Criteria

- o Familiar with the accounting and payroll software you use.
- o Accounting history or formal qualification.
- o Excellent written communication skills.

Assessment

- o Most software has a 'test company' set up, or you can register for a 30-day free trial with a mock company. Do this and have your shortlisted candidates set up mock employees and action a mock pay run. Have them complete a mock termination and payout as well.

Metrics

- o Pay run is completed on time each cycle, at least one day before payments are due to be processed.
- o An average of less than one pay issue per 20 staff per cycle. Staff will always tell you when they are underpaid. Always assume the same number have been overpaid and stayed quiet.

23. Timesheet Management

Result

Have your hourly rate employees' and contractors' timesheets managed, data entered and polished.

Summary

If you are still using paper-based timesheets, last decade would be a really good time to update your system. There are heaps of good apps that allow staff to clock on and off using their Smartphones. If you are all in the one office, spring for a cheap tablet and leave it near the office entrance. Most time apps on a tablet will capture a photo at sign in to avoid time-theft by employees.

If you are determined to stay in last century, outsourcing probably isn't for you, although you can always scan your timesheets, or maybe send them by fax or carrier pigeon, and have them manually data entered.

Even with digital timesheets captured in the cloud, there are always issues. People *forget* to sign in or out. They take leave, get sick, run errands and then head home.

You need to manage the timesheet data and polish it before you are ready to export to your payroll platform.

Have staff send notification of any 'mistakes' to a specific email address, different to your payments one. Have your remote staff member review and make changes, then notify you of these for verification.

You can also have them compile a spreadsheet of the timesheet infractions each cycle by each staff member. This will let you track the serial offenders and manage their performance better.

Have the remote staff member send you a spreadsheet showing issues and irregularities with the pay run for you to review prior to processing the payments.

Selection Criteria

- o Familiar with the timesheet app or software you use.
- o Accounting history or formal qualification.
- o Excellent written communication skills.

Assessment

- o Have them enter last cycle's timesheets again and compare them to the result you got.

Metrics

- o Timesheets are polished and ready at least one day before payments are due to be processed.
- o An average of less than one missed timesheet issue per 50 staff per cycle. Staff will always tell you when they are underpaid. Always assume the same number have been overpaid and stayed quiet.

24. Personnel File Management

Result

Keep all staff records compiled, up-to-date, ordered and digital.

Summary

Keeping all your staff records together is just good practice. However, finding the time to file every document, letter, doctor's note, performance appraisal and timesheet can be tedious.

So outsource it.

Set up a separate email address and every time you get an email, forward it. Every time you get physical correspondence, photograph it with your phone, or scan and email it. Your remote staff member will be able to see the name of the local staff member it relates to and file it accordingly.

You now have comprehensive, accessible staff files. Plus you never have to worry about leaving the filing cabinet unlocked and the wrong person getting up to mischief.

Selection Criteria

- o Ability to read and comprehend business correspondence.
- o Far enough removed from your workplace that privacy isn't a concern.

Metrics

- o All documents forwarded are correctly filed.

25. Roster Management

Result

Have your roster professionally scheduled. Have a contact person for any changes to go through.

Summary

Rostering is a painful, time-consuming job. It also leads to 'office politics' with the favourites and friends of the roster manager getting the cream of the shifts.

By outsourcing this, you save time and money and remove a major source of angst among your staff.

They now email in their un-availability, shift requests and leave requests. They can't curry favour or suck up.

If they want to change a shift, they can still find someone to swap with, but the change goes through the remote roster manager.

You set your weekly or fortnightly requirements for your remote staff member and let them roster as best available. By providing key data on your staff and historical rosters they will be able to see what is expected.

You should always sign off over the roster, but make it clear to all that you cannot make changes to the roster. You can, of course, order changes to be made, but keep that to yourself.

The roster can then be made available through an online link so all staff can see the most up-to-date roster. All staff should also be emailed when any roster comes out or is changed in a way that affects them.

Selection Criteria

- o Competence with the software package you use for rostering.
- o Excellent written communication skills.
- o Ability to understand complex diaries and rosters.

Assessment

- o Attach a previous roster, a blank roster, management notes for changed staffing levels required for the next cycle, and some staff requests for specific shifts. Have them submit a sample roster based on the previous roster and requested changes.

Metrics

- o Roster completed to management requirements so all shifts are covered.
- o Roster issued by required deadline.
- o On a scale of 1 to 10, all staff rate the rostering system and the remote staff member at an 8 or higher.

26. Staff Engagement Surveys

Result

Get solid feedback on how your staff are feeling, what they feel is working, and what they hate and want changed.

Summary

Use staff engagement surveys as an effective tool to quantify and begin to change that most difficult aspect of any company: the culture.

Have the remote staff member compile a list of 100 or more potential questions, then ask each key manager to choose 3-5 that they most want data on. I would then choose a similar number based on current initiatives and issues.

Have the remote staff member create an online survey with the chosen questions. Each staff member can then be sent a unique link to complete the survey. The remote staff member can see who hasn't completed the survey and follow up, or pass on to you to follow up.

Once the responses are in, you should get a summary of them, as well as an executive summary showing the key findings. Make sure the raw data is included as well, in case you need to go back to check anything.

Remember, having asked for feedback, you need to be

seen to act on it or you risk losing credibility with your staff.

Selection Criteria

- o Excellent written communication.
- o Proven research history.
- o Familiar with an online survey platform, or Google documents – simple and free.

Assessment

- o Have candidates create a simple 10-question survey and send through to you.

Metrics

- o Questions broadly researched and submitted.
- o Survey well-designed and laid out.
- o Responses followed up.
- o Results compiled in a logical and well-organised manner; executive summary accurately reflects the raw data.

27. Performance Reviews Management

Result

Questionnaires sent and responses received from all local staff, results collated and prepared for face-to-face performance reviews with local staff.

Summary

Performance reviews are an essential part of staff development, so why do so many of us hate them? Possibly because they chew up time and energy, but mostly we hate having tough conversations.

A typical performance review will involve:

- o Giving a self-questionnaire to the staff member.
- o Hassling them to complete it and return it.
- o The manager completing a similar questionnaire.
- o Comparing the 2 documents
- o A face-to-face discussion.

Well, you can outsource 80% of that.

Have a remote staff member develop or update the questionnaire to reflect current world's best practice. Issue it to each staff member, then have the remote staff member touch base with staff in between to make sure they are on track to complete and return it on time.

Use the NET concept with the remote staff member to complete the manager's component of the survey during a voice-call with you, or dictate your responses.

The remote staff member is to compare the 2 questionnaires and prepare a summary and report, noting any discrepancies.

Selection Criteria

The remote staff member will be communicating directly with your staff for a task essential to the staff member's growth and development. You want this process conducted professionally.

- o Clear and professional written communication.
- o Clear and professional voice communication.

Assessment

- o Clear, grammatical and professional application.
- o Shortlisted candidates to write a mock follow-up letter to a staff member who is late returning the questionnaire.
- o Conduct a phone interview, and expect them to be clear and well-spoken.

Metrics

- o Questionnaires updated professionally.
- o All staff questionnaires are returned on time.
- o Manager questionnaires filled in accurately.
- o Timely return of all comparisons and summaries.

28. Conduct a 360-degree Performance Review

Result

Complete a 360-degree performance review for each of your managers.

Summary

A 360-degree review assists a manager's development by showing them how they are viewed by their superiors, peers and subordinates.

It is an excellent tool to highlight management strengths and challenges or areas for improvement.

There are a number of excellent templates available. Have your remote staff member research and assemble questionnaires for each of the three groups.

Approve the questions then have them converted into online surveys and issued to all relevant staff with unique links.

Once all staff have completed their section of the review, have your remote staff member assimilate the results into three summary reviews.

Have the results submitted to a senior manager for vetting first. This is an essential safeguard for the mental wellbeing of the manager in question.

Have the results updated if necessary, then sent directly from the remote staff member to the manager undergoing the 360 review and their next up-manager simultaneously, as if no senior review has been conducted. The full review should be discussed with the staff member's immediate supervisor.

Selection Criteria

The remote staff member will be communicating directly with your staff for a task essential to the staff members' growth and development. You want this process conducted professionally.

- o Clear and professional written communication.
- o Clear and professional voice communication.

Assessment

- o Clear, grammatical and professional application.
- o Shortlisted candidates to write a mock follow-up letter to a staff member late returning questionnaire.
- o Conduct a phone interview, expect them to be clear and well-spoken.

Metrics

- o Questionnaires updated professionally.
- o All staff questionnaires are returned on time.
- o Manager questionnaires filled in accurately, following voice-call.

Recruitment

Result

Receive a shortlist of suitable candidates for an opening based on your specified criteria.

Summary

LinkedIn is a recruitment platform as much as a professional networking platform.

The profiles people post are frequently targeted to acquiring new employment opportunities. When you pay the premium content charges, you are able to access some powerful search features, as well as a considerable amount of information on candidates.

You will need to be quite specific about the candidate you are looking for. Generate a list of:

- o   Must haves.
- o   Should haves.
- o   Could haves.

This will give your recruiter an excellent base to sift and sort potential candidates, as well as being able to prioritise likely candidates.

Provide your remote recruiter with a position description, company information and employment sales kit. Authorise them to contact candidates to gauge interest.

You can also use LinkedIn to track previous work colleagues and make contact to verify work claims and style.

By the time the list hits your desk, you have a candidate shortlist that has expressed interest, been reference-checked and with proven relevant skills.

Selection Criteria

- o Has access to LinkedIn premium account.
- o History of successful recruitment and placement.

Metrics

- o Shortlist of at least five suitable candidates.
- o Provide full data on the approach and responses received.
- o Provide full reference response from at least five previous colleagues for each shortlisted candidate.

30. Resume Sorting

Result

Receive a sorted and prioritised shortlist of resumes based on the applications to a job ad.

Summary

If you have ever tried to recruit in a market that has a surplus of candidates, you will know the nightmare of trying to wade through hundreds of resumes to shortlist the right candidates. You need to move quickly, but don't want to discard the right candidate.

If you are able to set a series of hard-and-fast criteria by which to evaluate resumes, have the remote staff member use the 'must have, should have, could have' system to sort through them all.

Have the remote staff member eliminate all candidates who don't have all of the 'must haves', and at least half of the 'should haves'.

You can then have them score the remaining resumes based on a point system:

- o   3 points for every 'should have' requirement met.
- o   1 point for every 'could have' requirement met.

If it's still a close race with lots of candidates, add more criteria. If you have over 20 candidates with PhDs, lucky you. Have the candidate list submitted in priority order, based on points. Read the top resumes until you find 4-5 you want to interview.

Selection Criteria

o   Outstanding language comprehension skills. Look for candidates who rank in the top 20% of reading comprehension tests.
o   A recruitment history an advantage.

Metrics

o   Assess a few candidate resumes at random, verify that the points you award these resumes matches the points on the full prioritised list you receive.

31. Phone Screening

Result

Have shortlisted candidates phone-screened and questioned to verify that spoken, on-the-spot answers match their resume claims.

Summary

Everyone lies on their resume, it's just a matter of to what degree. You want to weed out those who blatantly and grievously spin bull dust.

Once you have shortlisted the best resumes, it can be a good idea to do some further investigation before you waste more time.

Calling someone without notice and asking for 5-10 minutes of their time to discuss the position they have applied for will usually get a positive response. If they can't talk then, ask what time they can be called back.

Even then, they will seldom prepare seriously for something that has been explained as a quick 5-10 minute chat, unlike a formal interview.

Have your remote staff member craft a list of potential questions. Review these and agree on 5-6 stock questions you want answered.

Allow the remote staff member to spend the rest of the time verifying claims made on the resume. Ask open-ended questions, e.g. "How long did you work at ABC Corporation?" or "What were your main responsibilities there?" "What was your greatest success there?"

This information will be on the tip of their tongue if they truly lived the experience they are claiming.

You may choose a summary and notes of the interview, a full transcription, or a recording.

(Make sure you understand your local telecommunications recording laws. Typically, you just have to inform them the call is being recorded).

Selection Criteria

- o Clear and professional spoken communication skills.
- o Ability to work during your normal business hours.

Assessment

- o Have them conduct a mock phone-screen with you and one of your staff.

Metrics

- o Conduct accurate phone-screens. Do a random call-back of a candidate to get their feedback on the phone screen.
- o Professional, concise and pertinent data reported

32. Interviewing

Result

Have a formal interview conducted via video-link, and receive an executive summary, full transcription and recording of the interview.

Summary

The more trouble a staff member has to go to in order to obtain a position, the more they value it. This means they work harder to keep it and succeed in it. It also increases your chance of getting the right candidate in the role.

It is good practice to conduct more than one interview. This is time consuming and can be repetitive if you have a small recruitment team. So get the first interview done remotely.

Have a remote staff member construct an interview script that you approve. Have them use email to book a time with each candidate you wish to interview.

Conduct the interview via video-link. You may wish to block your remote staff member's video feed, depending on where they are interviewing from.

Have the interview recorded and the file saved to your cloud storage. The remote staff member should provide you with an interview summary and opinion, along with the full recording.

Having a remote interview with an independent person gives you the chance to ask the same or similar questions to verify answers, without seeming vague or like you are wasting their time.

Selection Criteria

- o Exceptional spoken language skills.
- o Ability to understand a wide range of local spoken language and colloquialisms.
- o Ability to video-conference and record the feed.

Assessment

- o Have them conduct a mock interview with one of your staff members.

Metrics

- o Interviews conducted in a professional and appropriate manner.
- o Summary is an accurate reflection of the interview. An arbitrary number of interviews can be audited for verification.

33. Testing and Profiling

Result

Psychometric personality profile and aptitude test results on shortlisted candidates.

Summary

Psychometric personality profiling and aptitude testing is an incredibly powerful and accurate recruiting tool, provided it is done by the candidate.

You can ensure this by having the testing completed in your office, but this takes up staff time. It can be just as effective to conduct your tests online, with someone to administer the tests and verify the person completing the tests is your candidate.

Have your remote staff member prepare a list of possible tests to use and make your decision based on the skills, ability and profile required for each role.

Ideally, you will still coordinate a group of candidates to do the tests simultaneously, as this saves the remote staff member's time.

The candidates must have access to a computer with webcam and good internet connection.

Run the tests online with the candidate in front of the webcam and the remote staff member ensuring they are not receiving help or looking up answers online.

The remote staff member should also grade and standardise all test scores for you.

Selection Criteria

- o Spoken language skills to issue instructions.
- o Access to software that will allow multiple video conferences.
- o Great internet connection.

Metrics

- o Test results for all shortlisted candidates collated and submitted.
- o All test scores are correctly marked and standardised – audit one to authenticate.

34. Reference Checking

Result

Verify the work history and claims of a candidate you want to hire.

Summary

Reference checking is one of the most reliable, and hardest to fake, aspects of the recruitment process. This is gives you a chance to verify what you have been told in an interview.

A former employer will generally give you an honest read. If the candidate hasn't listed their most recent former, not current employer, ask why and then ask for the contact details of this employer.

Whilst the reference check can be faked, it takes a lot of skill and planning and I've yet to see it pulled off effectively.

The problem is that many employers don't do it! This is typically done at the end of the recruitment process when they have already decided to hire the candidate. So it makes sense not only to verify, but to have someone else verify.

Have your remote staff member generate a list of possible reference check interview questions. Refine these into a script with them.

Provide your remote staff member with a copy of the resume and interview notes so they can verify claims.

Have your remote staff member call the referee and record the call.

You should require a report on the reference as well as either a transcript of the call or a copy of the recording

(Make sure you know your local telecommunication laws if you are going to record.)

Selection Criteria

- o Fluent, clear and professional spoken language skills.
- o Ability to produce well-structured business reports.

Assessment

- o Conduct a voice interview with them to see how professionally they present on the phone.

Metrics

- o Reference checks completed in a timely manner during appropriate local business hours.
- o Report clear and accurate representation of the interview.
- o Scripted questions asked as well as resume and interview fact verification questions.

Marketing and Public Relations: Content Writing

35. Marketing Strategy

Result

Have a high-level marketing strategy, with a detailed implementation plan including all actions and timeframes.

Summary

A coordinated and planned marketing strategy is far more effective than ad hoc efforts. It also has the benefit of being systemised and repeatable.

Too often, businesses make the mistake of only marketing when they need more work. This results in a feast/famine repeating cycle. If you market consistently, even when you are flooded with work, you will have a consistent flow. At peak times, you will experience abundance and can select only the most lucrative contracts.

You need clarity about what you want to achieve, so make sure you can articulate your goals for sales and growth.

Give the remote marketer access to as much information about your business, your clientele, your staff and your areas of expertise as possible.

They will be able to propose a strategy that has a number of high-level points. If you agree with those, the remote marketer can proceed to fill in the details of the content marketing plan. This should include actions and dates, and identify the person responsible for making each action happen.

Once you have a strategy, you can engage other remote marketing specialists to create your content, images, articles and other marketing collateral.

Selection Criteria

- o Bachelor's degree in marketing or promotions.
- o Work history that shows experience with high-level marketing strategy creation or management.
- o Excellent written and spoken language skills.
- o You like them and can trust them.

Metrics

- o You receive a high-level marketing overview that shows an understanding of your business.
- o The actions on the implementation plan are in line with the brand of your business.
- o If they are going to handle the implementation and content creation as well, e.g. an agency, then set a verifiable growth target. For example, an increase in call enquiry volume of 25%.
  You need a way for the remote agency to verify the figures so they know you are being fair.

36. Articles - Summarise and Assimilate Existing Articles Into Unique Content

Result

A series of unique articles, containing concepts and ideas that have proven to appeal to your target audience, ready to be posted online as marketing collateral or PR content.

Summary

To create unique and seemingly-original content that is based on well-received and reviewed articles and content.

Let's face it, there is no such thing as an original idea. As the adage goes, 'there's nothing new under the sun'. As people, we are a construct of everything we have heard and learnt throughout our lives.

Take some of the best and most relevant content and provide it to them in a clear, concise and useable form.

Your remote staff member will have to read the articles you provide. You may have them do research and collect articles – you will need to provide specific guidelines for what content is relevant and desired. They will summarise articles, assimilate multiple sources of content and provide unique content that will pass online plagiarism checks.

Selection Criteria

- o Must have excellent grasp of the language you will be communicating in. They will need to understand concepts, assimilate meaning and rewrite it in an engaging way.
- o Creative writing ability.
- o Reading comprehension ability.
- o Have access to plagiarism-checking software or website

Assessment

- o Ask for samples of previously-created unique content.
- o Provide them with a short sample article to summarise into unique content.

Metrics

- o Produce agreed number of articles.
- o Each article is 400-600 words in length.
- o Each article passes top 3 online plagiarism checking tools as 95% unique content.

37. Articles – Create From Your Recorded Notes and Research

Result

Have a series of relevant, original articles based on spoken recordings made by you.

Summary

No one knows your business as well as you, right? So how do you leverage that knowledge so that you can market it without doing all the work yourself?

Use the concept of No Extra Time. When you are driving, walking, or lying in bed, grab a notepad and scribble some ideas about articles you would like to publish to promote your business.

Set your phone to voice record and speak on the topic for 5 minutes. It doesn't have to be well-ordered or structured, just pour out your knowledge and what you would like the article to include.

The remote staff member will listen to your recording, create a mind-map for the article, and research some similar articles and facts for reference to add credibility. Then they will write the article for you.

You now have a well-structured, well-researched and credibly-referenced article based on your ideas and your knowledge of your business, ready to post or blog in the medium of your choice.

Selection Criteria

- o Bachelor of journalism, writing or language, e.g. Bachelor of English Literature.
- o Able to understand your spoken recordings.
- o Excellent written language skills.
- o Understanding of structure and protocol for professional writing.

Assessment

- o Upload a sample of your spoken voice recording and have them turn this into a simple article.

Metrics

- o Articles are well-structured, clear, and flow in a logical and engaging way.
- o Article reflects your spoken content and intent.
- o Article contains references to credible sources.

38. Articles – Commentary

Result

Establish yourself and your business as a credible authority, in touch with the market and current events.

Summary

The world moves fast and attention spans are short. If you want to get noticed, make sure part of your strategy is to be in the thick of whatever topics are.

Use a staff member who has access to full versions of social media tracking software, to monitor topics that are in your sphere of influence or that affect or interest your target market. You will need to clearly define both of these to your staff member.

The staff member then writes commentary on the topic, or assists your audience to understand how it may affect them. This may involve criticism, praise or observation.

This is a long-term relationship type of gig. The person you are hiring is going to need to learn what you are interested in, your views and writing style, and your general opinions on the world and business.

Identify the places where you want the commentary to be posted, based on what the staff member may select as the manner of delivery.

Make sure the commentary is not formulated to reject

outright any opponents' view and that reasonable explanations are provided for disagreeing with any opponents' view.

Focus on building a foolproof editorial content on the basis of strong statistical data, relevant analogies and audience polls or reviews, where possible. Commentary is primarily meant for constructive criticism and should thus provide possible solutions/alternatives to the current mechanism in place.

Selection Criteria

- Ideally have a bachelor's degree in journalism or media.
- Should have strong command of the language in which the content is to be written.
- Review their previous work in their profile.

Assessment

- Conduct interviews to understand how aligned the writer is, to gauge their adaptability.
- Get them to provide commentary on a topic.

Metrics

- Relevant, concise and engaging content – require unlimited changes until you are satisfied.
- Word or page count – set required amount.

39. Blogging

Result

A blog that regularly has relevant and engaging content posted to it to promote your organisation.

Summary

We have all heard blogging helps promote our brand, keeps our organisation relevant and helps with our search engine ranking. Many of us have even tried it. It takes significant time and discipline to consistently produce and post content.

One of the biggest mistakes people make in blogging is to create a great stream of content that draws in followers, then stop's for a month or longer. The followers soon drop off and forget about the brand.

In order for a blog to be successful, you need to feed it consistently. So set up a system that makes this happen?

Decide on the theme of your blog and write half a dozen posts yourself. Be specific and concise about your target audience and the sphere of influence you wish to establish credibility in. Having this to reference will be the guiding lights for your outsourced blogging team.

Engage a content writer/researcher who uses a Social Media Management tool. Have them monitor topics that trend in your area. They can then create articles based around trending topics, historical posts, world's best practice, and new ideas. Have them send you the topic of a blog and an outline before they start working.

Once they write the post, you get final approval before it goes live. If you are going away or going to be busy, have a bank of posts prepared and pre-approved by you.

Selection Criteria

- o Ability to write creative and engaging content.
- o Ability to research and understand your organisation and style.
- o Ability to understand your voice recordings.

Assessment

- o Have them produce a sample post on a set topic based on 3-4 key criteria.

Metrics

- o Idea outlines are submitted prior to writing the blog.
- o Blog posts of a specified length and content are sent for approval.
- o Articles are posted to the blog at the agreed frequency.
- o You can pay per post or by set number of words.
- o Negotiate to have the articles summarised to different lengths for different media – you can post elsewhere and link back to your blog.

40. Web Content

Result

Have well-structured and captivating content for your webpage.

Summary

Writing about ourselves or our organisations can be hard. Often what we do and take for granted, others find remarkable. The things we think make us great may just be icing on the delicious and enticing cake. No one buys just icing alone.

Make a bullet-point list of everything you do. Make a list of all your achievements as an organisation. Make a list of the skills and history of the executive management team.

Provide this to a remote creative writer. Have them plan a site-map for your website with a quick description of how they want to populate each page and the keywords they feel should be associated with each page.

Once you approve this, they can begin writing the content. Have them start on the least important pages first and submit each page as they finish it. This way you will be able to polish their style to suit the voice you want your organisation to use.

By the time they are crafting your landing page content,

you will have exceptional content.

Selection Criteria

- o Have written content for organisations in similar fields before.
- o Read their sample content, is it interesting? Does it grab your interest? Is it well-structured?
- o Look for writers who have written content across a broad range of industries, as this will demonstrate their ability to research and adapt.

Metrics

- o Site-map and keyword plan submitted shows a good grasp of your business and what you want to communicate.
- o Each page that comes in is written in a professional style and with the tone you want to have speaking for your company.
- o Each page that comes in is better than the last.
- o Set up payment milestones for the site–map and then each page. If things aren't on track as it progresses, you can stop at the last completed milestone

41. Proofreading

Result

Ensures a professional and well-structured document is issued from your business.

Summary

Proofreading is very essential for business, as right is always quiet but wrong is very loud. Sending out documents, reports and other content which have typos or grammatical errors can hamper your reputation.

Make sure your proofreader understands the scope of work to be covered as proofreading is different from editing. Inform the proofreader about what is required, i.e. final editing which involves checking for typing mistakes, punctuation/word processing errors such as repeated phrases or omitted lines, inconsistency in layout, formatting, referencing etc. or language correction, which involves correction of errors in grammar, vocabulary, sentence structure or expression.

Inform your proofreader about the target audience. In the case of proofreading documents written in the English language, the proofreader should know which English dictionary to refer to: UK English or US English, according to your preference and the function and target audience of the document.

The delivery date of the proofed document should

clearly be communicated to the proofreader so that the document could be received well in advance for any further changes to be incorporated in the document.

Though a fresh pair of eyes is always good, in the case of documents of high importance, it would be safer to appoint a professional proofreader.

Selection Criteria

- o Skilled in written English or the language in which document is to be proofread.
- o Knows your software
- o Good at communication and writing skills; expresses themselves clearly and professionally on their proposal and their biography page.

Assessment

- o Ask for portfolio of projects they have worked on.
- o Look out for good references or positive client feedback.
- o Provide a sample of your work to the proofreader to evaluate whether they are best suited for you.

Metrics

- o 100% error-free copy returned.
- o Drop in a few deliberate errors as checks to make sure they are picked up.

42. Press Release Writing

Result

Have a professional press release about your organisation constructed to produce maximum chances of being picked up by media organisations.

Summary

Being featured in the media can be a great way to promote yourself or your business. You just have to get a journalist to feature you.

This is the sort of project that works really well with a team effort.

1) Get the content. You can use web content, articles, blog posts, any original content that you wrote or have had written.

2) Get a journalist who provides freelance or outsourced services to sculpt the article into a press release. If they are in your country, or a country with a similar media landscape, they are more likely to be able to draft it with maximum chance of being picked up.

3) Have a researcher assemble a list of media contacts from media sources you would like to be featured in.

4) Have a media or social media expert track the topics that are currently trending in the media.

When something that fits you is identified, issue the press releases quickly to the relevant contact from your database.

Selection Criteria

- o Content Writer – see sections on Articles.
- o Journalist to act as Developmental Editor for the articles:
    - Currently or recently working as a journalist.
    - Based in a country with similar media landscape to yours.
    - Offers reasonably-priced editing services.
- o Media contacts – see 'Research' section.
- o Media expert:
    - Access to software that tracks your local media and social media topics.
    - Access to a summary news service.

Metrics

- o Journalist: Articles are picked up by at least 25% of the media organisations you issue them to.
- o Media Expert: Relevant content articles are issued to appropriate media agencies regularly.

43. Competition and Awards Applications

Result

Have a polished and bespoke award or competition application completed, without wasting days of your life.

Summary

Winning awards is fantastic marketing. The process can be harrowing, involved and chew up days of your precious time.

Chances are that if you have done this before, you are keen to avoid repeating the experience. If you have entered awards before, you have also laid out your best points before.

If you are able to pull together old applications, as well as giving a remote staff member access to as much data on yourself or your organisation as possible, they will be well on their way to reformatting the information in a unique way for the award application.

Once you have the application, send it straight on to the staff member. Let them assess it and see what they think they can complete and what they think they will need more information on.

Have them send you a bulleted list of questions or requests for information. You can either write replies or simply dictate your responses.

By passing on the information, rather than answering the specific questions yourself, you empower the staff member to answer all the questions.

You also save yourself time and avoid the common staff issue of having all the tough questions thrown at you to handle. If they know they will end up answering them anyway, they are more likely to give it a go.

Selection Criteria

- o Ability to write in a professional and engaging style.
- o Ability to research and compile information.

Assessment

- o A written assessment on a topic you nominate.
- o Consider a professional test on 'abstract reasoning'. This tests the ability to draw accurate conclusions from limited information.

Metrics

- o Thorough, complete and professional award or competition application completed.

    If you are unhappy with a section, send it back with notes until it is completed.

eMarketing

Result

Have a series of articles that are relevant to your clients and contacts.

Summary

For an eNewsletter to work, the people you send it to need to read it. If you just talk about yourself and your company, only you, your staff and family will read it. Guess what? They already buy from you!

So you need to find topics that are of interest to your target audience. If you can collate a series of articles that are loosely based around your industry or area of knowledge and provide interesting, topical content, you have something people will read.

The email will come from you and you can stick your logo on the top and an ad for your company in the guts of it. This will promote your company whilst showing you are industry leaders who keep up with and set trends.

Set your remote researcher to collect articles on topics relevant to you. In the simplest form, you will put a one paragraph lead-in to each article of interest that is found. If your readers are interested, they can click through to the page that the original article is on. This is a useful service, as you are locating and directing your readers to relevant and fascinating content.

If you want to take it a step further, you can have the remote researcher collect articles and write them into original content to post on your page (see sections on Articles).

Selection Criteria

o   Ability to understand your company and industry. Look for a remote worker who has worked across a wide range of industries, as this is usually a sign of versatility.
o   High level written communication skills.

Assessment

o   Have them locate 2 relevant articles for your business and send through links.

Metrics

o   At least 50% of the articles collected are relevant and useable for your eNewsletter.
o   If writing original content, ensure it passes an online plagiarism check.

45. Email Marketing Creation

Result

Have an email for your marketing campaign that gets at least double your industry rate of click-throughs.

Summary

It is estimated that 98% of the email traffic in the world is spam. With that level to contend with, you need to:

1) Make sure your email address is not black-listed or marked as spam, or none of your correspondence will ever get through again.
2) Ensure that yours stands out enough to be read and considered by at least twice as many readers as your competition.

To achieve these things takes some thought and planning. You need to start with the name it is sent from, then the subject line. What is the first text line they see if they click on it? Most email programs won't download pictures at first to save bandwidth. The reader needs to click to download images. Is the first line, then paragraph, enough to hook the reader in, get them to download the full email and keep reading?

No matter how good your content, it is worth getting an experienced email marketer to develop the layout and design of your campaign. They should also be able to guide you on the best time to send the campaign out to your readers.

Having said that, as long as they don't unsubscribe or block your email or domain, it is still a win. The name of the game is to get your brand in front of them frequently. So anything less than total rejection will achieve that. It may sit in their inbox until a day when they need your services.

Selection Criteria

- o Experience with email marketing campaigns.
- o Look at their work history. Are the emails they design easy to read? How would they look before images are loaded?
- o What is their feedback score from previous clients?

Metrics

- o Price per campaign, so you can always discontinue if it isn't working.
- o Use an online email marketing platform that they have access to. Require that click-throughs are at least double the industry average and unsubscribes are less than 3% from contacts you have sent to previously or 10% of cold contacts.

46. Audio and Video Editing

Result

Combines multiple videos and images to create a new video; trim, lengthen and cut clips, adds approved music to your videos, special effects to videos as per your specification, clears background noise from audio clips, additional time to you to create more content, short movies, documentaries, etc.

Summary

Though you can edit audios and videos yourself with software available online, it is slow and time-consuming. Hiring a video or audio editor who would convert your raw recorded material into a finished product by combining the pieces, editing it, adding sound and other special effects.

To get the desired result, provide the video and/or audio editor with the following:

o   All raw footages, along with camera shots which need to be assembled. For audio editing, provide the voice notes to be combined to make a single audio piece.

o   Brief them on the outline, the script, the purpose and the target audience for whom the video/audio clip is to be prepared.

o   In case you want commentaries or banners in the

video clips, provide the content of the commentary and specify the places where commentaries should appear.

o Provide the background score to be added to the video/audio clip.

Review the first cut of the edited video or audio clip for further tweaking and to ensure logical and smooth running of the video or audio. Suggest any changes. Negotiate unlimited changes into the contract.

Selection Criteria

- o Previous projects using appropriate software.
- o You like their previous work samples.
- o Dedicated and able to work under pressure and strict deadlines.

Assessment

- o Give them a small piece of audio or video to edit to assess their proficiency and level of understanding of work.

Metrics

- o Flowing and flawless audio and video.
- o You love it. You have unlimited changes, so keep going until you love it. This is subjective but important.
- o Completed within timeframe.

47. Animation

Result

Your concept video is professionally designed, edited and includes all audio in sync with images.

Summary

Whilst being the star of your own video can be appealing, it is not always the best idea. Actors are expensive and come with demands and needs.

Animation can be an awesome way to get your point across with minimal cost.

Start with your concept and brainstorm what you want to achieve. If you are creatively impaired, you can simply post the outline of what you want to achieve and ask for proposals. Allow your remote teams to come up with concepts for you to complete the objectives effectively.

If you have something more specific in mind, you will need to develop the plot, characters and script. Make sure you give as detailed a description as you can about each aspect.

Create milestones around each step of the project and ensure you give prompt and useful feedback and suggestions.

There should be unlimited changes included until you have the outcome you want.

Selection Criteria

- o   They have worked on similar projects before and received top feedback.
- o   View their previous animation projects and ensure it matches the quality and message you want to convey.
- o   Make sure they understand your requirements.

Metrics

- o   Animation is smooth and seamless, not jerky.
- o   Sound is completely in sync with the images.
- o   The tone of the audio is correct for your message.
- o   The whole project is 'on-brand' for your company.

48. Video Subtitling

Result

Have your video subtitled for the hearing-impaired and for foreign language distribution.

Summary

Having subtitles on your videos, or as options on your videos, increases your possible market penetration. It can also show you care for disadvantaged groups, if it is subtitled in the same language as the video.

The first step is to get a transcript of the video. This can be done by the same remote staff member, or you may choose to have a separate staff member type up the transcript.

The remote staff member will then edit the video to add the subtitles. Make sure you specify the text colour and font to keep it on-brand.

The subtitle text should not take up more than 20% of the screen at any time and must flow naturally with the video.

Selection Criteria

- o Familiar with a suitable video editing software.
- o Able to understand the language and vocabulary used in the video. They must be able to follow the

video to make the subtitles flow effectively.

Metrics

- ○ Subtitles are accurate and complete
- ○ Subtitles flow with the video. Give it to someone who hasn't seen it and have them watch it without sound. Does the flow of the subtitles allow them to watch along successfully and enjoyably?

Traditional Marketing

49. Logo Designing

Result

Get a standout and professional logo that will attract customers to your business.

Summary

A professional logo can make your business stand out from the crowd.

Educate the designer on your interpretation of the brand and the message that you want the logo to send. Give them information on your business, background and target customers.

A logo should be simple, memorable, versatile and appropriate for your business. Make sure you spell these out to the designer. Suggest the designers to stay away from clichés and encourage them to come up with something original.

Make sure the designer does in-depth research of your business to create a unique logo. Review a few sketches with the designer before you settle on the final logo which truly defines your business.

Communicate the deadline and keep in regular touch with the designer throughout the course to ensure that deadline is not missed.

Discuss the transfer of ownership of the Logo design with

the designer upfront and move ahead with the one who could transfer all rights without any hesitation.

Most designers will provide you with 5-10 sample logos. Review and pick the ones you most like and have them develop those until you have a logo that is perfect. Rebranding is expensive, so make sure you take the time to get it right first time!

Selection Criteria

- o Should have excellent knowledge of graphic design software such as Adobe Illustrator and Photoshop.
- o Opt for a designer who listens to your needs and understands your taste.
- o You love their previous designs.
- o Look for a designer who asks more questions about your business, or who has visited your website and shows they understand who you are and what you want.

Metrics

- o A unique logo which you feel conveys your business message.
- o Positive feedback from your existing clients.
- o Supportive customer care service post-completion of project.

50. Graphic Design

Result

Images and layout that are captivating and 'on-brand' for your company.

Summary

Graphic design for your marketing material is essential to capture the attention of your target audience long enough to get your message across.

The best content in the world is lost to a cluttered, ugly layout with clashing colours and lousy image design.

Unfortunately, graphic design is time-consuming and costly. This makes it ideal to outsource!

Start with the design brief.

- o   The title of your project.
- o   When and how you want it delivered.
- o   Provide any existing designs or logos you have, to ensure they marry this with your brand.
- o   Include any calls-to-action or headlines that you want incorporated in the design.

Make sure the graphic designer sends you proofs of the work as it progresses. If you see how it is developing, you can make the changes you want as you go along. This is the surest way to end up with a product you are happy with.

Selection Criteria

- o You like and are captivated by their previous work.
- o Pick someone with a work history that most matches your brand image.
- o Make sure their skills include the use of professional design software.

Metrics

- o Incorporate unlimited changes into the contract. If you are not getting what you want, direct them back to the work history that attracted you to them in the first place.
- o You have an original, captivating and well laid-out design that matches your brand and your message.

51. Marketing Collateral

Result

Marketing collateral that you are ready to proudly distribute for your company.

Summary

Some of the marketing collateral you may want to have created for your company:

- Fact sheets on your company or a product/service.
- Biographies of staff and management.
- Company background.
- Project or work history and milestones achieved.
- Brochures, pamphlets and booklets.
- Annual reports.
- Catalogues.

The form it takes depends on your business.

Most of the marketing collateral you produce will need input from 2 main contributors:

1) Content writers.
2) Graphic designers.

By successfully incorporating these two staff skillsets, you can create brilliant marketing collateral to fill just about any of your print needs within your company.

A lot of offshore companies will have a team that

incorporates these two complimentary skillsets. You may prefer to engage an agency or team who can drive the process from start to finish.

Selection Criteria

- o You like the writing style and genre of the previous work they have done.
- o Their writing is professional and suits the voice you want to use for your company.
- o The layout and design of previously-completed projects is engaging and memorable.

Metrics

- o Marketing collateral is written professionally and is relevant, on-brand and conveys your message.
- o Layout incorporates your logos and colour design scheme.
- o Layout and content are original and unique.

52. Copywriting

Result

Captivating, concise copy that grabs your attention and imagination.

Summary

Good copywriting alters your perspective on a topic. It engages you and makes you take a fresh look at something. It draws you in and captures your attention and imagination.

Copywriting is short and concise, not lengthy content. It is a tag-line, a billboard, or a one- or two-line ad.

Good copywriting must have a great 'lead'. It must have an opening line that hooks you and makes you want to keep reading.

It must be simple and avoid jargon and clichés. It must be targeted at your audience and address their needs. It must cut out excess and boil down your message into the fewest words possible.

You are going to have to pay someone to get to know your brand, your message, your market positioning. Then you are only going to get a line or two in return.

Be ready and accept this. Just make sure you get the line you want. You can always have multiple options submitted and choose or work with the best of them.

Selection Criteria

- o Look at their previous work:
    - Do you want to know more about each topic?
    - Do you want to read more because it is short and funny?
    - Does it make you smile?
    - Is it professional and well-crafted?
- o Copywriting is an art and difficult to teach or learn, so look for someone with the gift.

Metrics

- o The copy has a great lead-in.
- o It is short and inspiring, grabs your attention and makes you want to read more.
- o It is on-brand and on-message.

53. Business Card Design

Result

Have a professional, well-laid out business card that succinctly displays your essential information.

Summary

Your business card is usually the first thing a prospect or contact gets when they meet you. Short of your clothes and haircut, it is the major thing you can control that they will judge you on.

It will also be the memento they take to remember you.

It's sounding pretty important about now.

Having your business card matching your image and brand is essential, or matching what you would like it to be. If your card is cheap and poorly thought-out, they will assume that your approach to business and life is the same.

Decide what you want on your card. Do you really need to give every single way they can possibly connect with you, every phone, landline, email, fax, 5 social media accounts and your address?

Do you want your logo and tagline on there? Do you just want to throw it all out there and see what looks good?

Make sure you negotiate unlimited changes so that you end up with the result you want. This is super important.

Take the time to get it right.

Selection Criteria

- o Look at the business card layouts and designs they have completed previously. If you see ones you like and that match your ideal brand and image, shortlist those. Someone used to a classic or a gothic style is not going to easily start using a very contemporary design. Pick someone who is designing in the space you want to occupy.

Metrics

- o You get a business card you love and want to show off. If you are getting frustrated, tell them. Ask them to go back a few designs if it has taken a wrong turn. You need to get it right.

Social Media

54. Photoshop

Result

Have your photo turned into a super professional-looking image with clean, uncluttered background and 'enhanced' foreground subject.

Summary

Have you seen what a professional photographer charges recently? One photo-shoot would exceed my entire costs for the publication and marketing of this book!

So how do you get that professional photo-shoot feel from an image you snapped on your phone? Easy. Cheat.

Your phone, like most modern digital cameras, has resolution and capture properties that match that used by most professional photographers. They can't afford to update as often as you change phones! So you already have a high resolution, HD image as a starting point.

Decide what you want to promote. You may want your main subject to dominate, so you can have the background altered, removed, or just 'blurred' to appear out of focus.

You may want to look flawless and 20 pounds lighter. You may want to remove someone from the shot or highlight a product that is somewhere in the shot.

You need to be clear about what your purpose is in getting the image photoshopped, if you are going to achieve the result you want. So take the time to get clarity.

Make sure you effectively communicate this to your remote photo alteration expert. They can do amazing things that would take too long to explain. Trust their expertise and just give them a solid brief.

Selection Criteria

- o View their work history of before and after shots. Make sure you see the sort of highlights and improvements you are after.
- o Make sure they are willing to do unlimited alterations until you are satisfied.

Metrics

- o A photo that is enhanced and improved in line with your specified criteria.
- o Photo does not appear altered or faked.
- o Changes flawlessly integrated with the original image.

55. Social Media – Written Content

Result

Written content that is appealing and relevant to the social media platform where it is posted.

Summary

There are more social media platforms than dinner plates in my cupboard. I spent years learning about the guests I would invite to a dinner party. I don't have that sort of time to devote to learning about each social media platform.

So I contract experts whose job it is to use, track and create content for social media. They spend their time learning about each platform and what works best, what attracts attention and comment.

This is important, as you don't just want to go with the social media you know and understand, plus it evolves quickly – once something works, everyone does it, so it stops working.

Have a SM content writer and editor who can take your articles, ideas and blog posts, and spin them into content that can attract the most attention.

Make sure they using the full professional versions of social media tracking and analytics software so they can give you solid feedback and data on how your post does in comparison with the rest of the market.

Selection Criteria

- o Access to full version of a social media tracking and analytics software.
- o Fluent across multiple social media platforms.
- o Ideally they should be a thought-leader or influencer with significant following on several platforms.

Assessment

- o Have them mould a short article into a social media post. Post it to your social media and see if it trends higher than your average posts.

Metrics

- o You have SM content that gets attention and comments above your historical average.
- o You are able to see results from the analytics-tracking package.

56. Social Media – Image Content

Result

Have images for your social media post that grab viewers' attention and drive comments and likes.

Summary

Most people have several social media accounts, frequently with cluttered news feeds. As they scroll through their home page, they will most often look for images, not headlines.

So you need to grab them with the image first, then hook them deep with your headline and first sentence.

Having the time to create images, illustrations or find and alter photos is often a struggle. So find someone competent who can do it for you.

Create your post, headline and lead sentence, or have it created for you. Send this to your image controller to have them fashion an image that suits your content whilst snatching the attention of the casual browser.

The image must be low cost and not infringe copyright. It must fit your brand and image, as well as the post.

They must be able to deliver in a short timeframe, usually within 12 hours. There is no point having an amazing post for a topic that is trending massively, only to find that when you get your image in a week you are on the tail end of a flooded topic that has been talked to death.

Selection Criteria

- o Has a work history that shows humorous, original, engaging images.
- o Is willing to sign over all rights to the image to you.
- o Has feedback showing they can work to a deadline.

Assessment

- o Provide a sample post. Have applicants submit an image they feel best suits the post.

Metrics

- o Image either does not appear elsewhere on the internet, e.g. Google picture search, or they can establish that you have the right to use it.
- o Image does not conflict with your brand or profile.
- o Image is on-message and appealing.
- o Image consistently provided within 12 hours of being provided with content.

57. Twitter Content Summariser

Result

Have blogs, articles and social media posts quickly turned into less than 140-character Twitter comments that produce retweets and clicks.

Summary

Twitter is a great medium for brevity. You don't have space to waffle on; you have to come straight to the point.

The problem is, how do you take that beautifully written and well-structured article and summarise it in a maximum of 140 characters?

This is very similar to copywriting, except you need it done quickly and consistently. There is rarely the time for lots of changes and fine-tuning.

Nonetheless, post the job under the banner and skillset of copywriting, as these are the people you need. If you have a copywriter you use, ask them if they have any experience with Twitter posts.

Twitter posts are a more specialised subset, as they require a different language or character set, using word shortcuts: 'with' becomes 'w/', dropping vowels from words, using contractions, symbols that don't clash with Twitter functionality and omitting unnecessary words.

The Twitter feed is more about conveying the message and less about the word-smithing to create a memorable phrase.

Selection Criteria

- o Look at their previous work, it won't take long:
    - - Do you want to know more about each topic?
    - - Do you want to read more because it is quick and fun?
    - - Does it make you smile?
    - - Is it professional and well-crafted?
- o Look for copywriting experience.

Metrics

- o Starts with a gripping lead-in.
- o Grabs your attention and makes you want to read more.
- o Communicates the heart and point of the article.
- o Generates specified number of retweets and click-throughs.

58. Social Media Management

Result

Manage all your social media accounts, post articles according to your content marketing plan and keep your team abreast of trending topics within your areas of influence and expertise.

Summary

Keeping social media content relevant and posting consistently is essential to maintaining a strong following.

One of the biggest mistakes people make with social media is to let their followers forget about them and their brand by not staying relevant and regular in their posts.

Define the area you want to be influential in. Remember the lesson Steve Jobs taught the world: Inventory Management. You may have a broad knowledge, but you should pick the areas you want to focus on. Be specific and concise about who your target audience is. Clarifying this will be the guiding premise for your SMM.

You need to arm your SMM with a bank of articles to post or contact details for your content writer so that they get them as needed. Remember – post consistently. If you are targeting a specific outcome, make sure your SMM has your content marketing plan.

Your SMM will also monitor topics that trend in your area of expertise. They will then flag the topic and some high view articles to your content writer. Your content writer can formulate a relevant post, send it to you for approval, then to your SMM to post across your various accounts as appropriate.

Once this is working well, you will be established as a thought-leader in your industry. Frequent posting means you will always have current contact with people and be at the forefront of their minds.

Selection Criteria

- o Access to a full version of a credible social media tracking tool.
- o Ability to communicate effectively with you and your content writer.
- o You trust them with your social media accounts.

Assessment

- o Have them produce a report on what is trending in your field today.

Metrics

- o Consistent posts across all your social media accounts.
- o Posts are appropriate to each platform.
- o Regularly provides reports on your industry trends and the performance of your posts.

59. Content Moderation and Online Reputation Management

Result

Protect your brand and reputation on all online forums and platforms.

Summary

'It takes 20 years to build a reputation, and 5 minutes to ruin it.'

Warren Buffet

The era of social media and online forums has empowered consumers. Now when someone isn't happy, they can all too quickly tell the world.

Of course, people are far more motivated to tell of their bad experiences then their good. So when that nightmare customer runs across Grumpy Joe on a bad day, you have a problem.

You should design a crisis management plan for dealing with such situations. Then you need to be ready to activate it.

Content moderation requires round-the-clock monitoring, ordinarily a costly process that is made significantly cheaper by outsourcing.

With some content, you may be able to remove negative

comments or posts, or request that they be taken down.

With other platforms, you will need to swing your crisis management plan into action to respond quickly in an appropriate way.

Many content management providers will have templates for you to use to create your crisis plan, so it becomes a lot easier to formulate your contingency planning.

Selection Criteria

- o Top level language skills.
- o An understanding of local slang terms.
- o Trained and briefed on your response plan.
- o Able to get in touch with you directly and quickly if the situation requires it.

Metrics

- o Any negative content posted about your company is immediately flagged.
- o Correct action is taken in accordance with the content crisis management plan.
- o Action is initiated within 15 minutes of the post.

Sales

60. Sales Calls

Result

Have a dedicated team who are able to consistently call prospective and current clients to generate hot leads or hard sales.

Summary

More leads and sales is something every business needs. We often shy away from 'telemarketing' because we hate it personally.

Whilst you can use the traditional telemarketing model, you need to do it carefully so you don't damage your brand or fall foul of local laws.

A more effective way to use sales calls can be to call:

- o Prospective clients who have expressed some interest in the past.
- o Lapsed clients who have bought from you before, but may have forgotten just how great you are.
- o Current clients who you want to see buying again.

Contacting people who know you as part of your ongoing sales and marketing strategy is just good sense. You want to use a range of contact mediums; if you just rely on email you will miss a large chunk.

You also don't want to push the 'pester balance' and contact them the same way too often. Yet, calls are time

174

consuming.

By outsourcing these 'touch base' and 'upsell' calls, you can save your local staff time and yourself, money.

You are probably best paying slightly more and engaging an offshore call centre for this; they come in all sizes now.

Make sure they record all the calls and keep a log.

Ensure you approve any scripts and define how much flexibility you want. Make sure the callers can speak your language naturally and with minimal accent.

Selection Criteria

- o Go for an established call centre that is of the right size, so your contract will be something they care about.
- o Ensure they record all calls and give you access to the call logs and recordings.

Assessment

- o Have them conduct several mock calls with your staff, family and friends.

Metrics

- o You get an increase in leads and sales.
- o You do NOT get complaints.
- o Do random surveys of people contacted to see how they felt about the way the call was handled.

61. Follow-up Calls

Result

Have all your sales presentations followed up regularly to ensure potential customers have all the information they need to make a decision to buy.

Summary

Most people and companies put all their effort into the sales presentation, however that may look. The problem is, customers may hear from several possible companies, then discuss privately before making a decision.

It is during this period of indecision that you want to get as busy as possible. You want your company to own the indecision period.

You can simply contact the client regularly to see how they are going and ask if they need any more information. This is a bit like the sales assistant coming up and asking, "May I help you?" Most people just answer, "No," which is the response they wanted anyway.

A better way is to keep some key features and benefits up your sleeve, or to promise to get back to them to answer some of their questions.

Having a member of your staff call to provide additional information re-engages your potential customer in your product or service.

Make up a list of key features, how they will benefit the customer and how they will make the customer feel. Turn these into phone scripts or talking points.

Now that it's systemised, it doesn't matter who makes the calls, so you may as well outsource it!

Selection Criteria

- o Fluent spoken language skills.
- o Ability to work from notes or a phone script.
- o Can readily work during your local business hours.

Assessment

- o Conduct a phone-screen to assess language skills.
- o Have them conduct a mock follow-up call from your script.

Metrics

- o All potential customers followed up within the specified timeframes.
- o Increase in customer engagement and sales.

62. Appointment Booking

Result

Have warm and hot leads followed up, and appointments booked for sales calls.

Summary

Following up warm and hot leads is an essential part of any sales process. Unfortunately, it can drag out, as people start asking a lot of questions for information that you will need to repeat during the presentation.

Having someone book these appointments saves you time and allows you to bring up the information as you have planned, in your well-rehearsed sales presentation. It also comes across as well-organised and professional, demonstrating that your business is an organisation big enough to be trusted with systems in place to deal with every little detail.

With a list of contacts, access to Google Maps, your online diary and a script or talking points, it is a very simple job to train someone to make these calls.

You don't need to train them extensively on your product or service, as you give them the fallback line that they are just your assistant making the appointment at a time to best suit the client. "What time would best suit you, sir/ma'am?"

Ensure that your travel is minimised and time between kept to suitable margins for travel and traffic. Google Maps allow you to select the time of trip to estimate traffic.

Remote staff can also call the day before the appointment to confirm.

Selection Criteria

- o Professional spoken language skills.
- o Able to use your appointment software.
- o Can work during your business hours; lives in a time zone relatively closely aligned to your own.

Assessment

- o Conduct phone interview.
- o Have them do a mock appointment booking call with a member of your staff or family.

Metrics

- o All leads followed up within a specified time period.
- o Appointments confirmed 24 hours prior.
- o Travel minimised and appointments back to back, where possible.
- o Feedback from clients at sales presentation is that the caller was professional, helpful and accommodating.

63. Proposal Writing

Result

Complete a detailed sales proposal for a potential customer based on information collected.

Summary

Whether following up a sales presentation or from information captured through an online form, a detailed and personalised proposal is of great assistance in closing the sale.

Create a process to turn the captured data into a professional-looking document that can be sent through to your potential customer.

Writing it so that it is personalised and doesn't feel like a standard mail merge generally means including a human being in the process.

Outsource this task and then have it printed and mailed locally, as well as emailed.

This generates a few additional opportunities:

1) A call to confirm they have received the email and to book a time for the salesperson to call them and go through it.
2) The call from the sales person to go through it.
3) You can also follow-up to ensure they got the physical copy and see if they need the

salesperson to call again to answer further questions.

Polite, meaningful follow-up is all designed to show you are a professional and systemised company that can be trusted to purchase from.

Selection Criteria

- o Creative and abstract writing skills.
- o Ability to present and structure a document professionally.

Assessment

- o Base your decision on whether the candidates have taken the time to personalise the proposal they put in. Many will work off a pro-forma document or at least large amounts of copy and paste. Does it feel generic or personal?

Metrics

- o Proposals completed within 48 hours of sales call, or within 12 hours of online form being completed.
- o Documents are well structured, grammatically correct and follow professional protocols.
- o Documents are personalised and flow naturally.

Customer Service

64. Chat Support

Result

Have a real staff member available to answer 'chat' questions from your customers 24/7.

Summary

This is an incredible tool that screams 'Big Company'. Having staff available 24/7, or 24/5 if you prefer, is a great customer service tool.

You don't need to pay remote staff to sit and wait for enquiries. You simply pay them to be on standby to answer the chat questions as the come in.

Pay then works on a per-enquiry basis, with a sliding scale of payment depending on how many seconds it takes them to get to the chat enquiry.

You will need to provide some basic training on your product or service. The advantage of chat support is that conversations are slightly delayed. If you pick someone who can type quickly and who has a two-screen setup, they can reference your manual and troubleshooting guide as they go.

The manual can be written or developed from chat or telephone support calls completed by local, fully trained staff. Simply record the call and screen of the local support person, and have this transcribed and made into a manual. Outsource this, obviously.

Selection Criteria

- o Ability to be on standby for chat conversations to start.
- o Able to access and cross-reference information rapidly.
- o Able to 'think on the run'.

Assessment

- o Interview them via a chat room, send them a document during the interview and start asking them questions about it. See how quickly they can find and type the correct answers.

Metrics

- o Chat enquiries answered in an average of 15 seconds.
- o 98% of chat enquiries answered within 60 seconds.
- o 90%+ of customer queries resolved during the chat support session.
- o Feedback rating of 8-10 for the chat support staff member.

65. Call Centre Support

Result

Having trained staff who can answer client enquiries and give a reasonable level of support. Able to book additional support calls as needed.

Summary

Having staff members who are able to take a call rather than an automated menu system is always a plus for any business.

Make sure you have a VOIP system in your office so you can divert calls offshore. They can always transfer the calls back to the local office through the VOIP system without the customer ever knowing.

You will need to create a basic training manual for the phone staff. This can be readily created by recording customer calls over a period of time. Catalogue and describe the calls, then you can get the relevant calls transcribed and create scripts around these.

Use the product information you have already documented as the base for your training information. Website, sales documents, manuals and fact sheets are great starting points to create systems for support staff.

It is worth looking into an offshore call centre that can guarantee rates for training and calls. If the staff member you spent time training leaves, they will be responsible for training the replacement. Make sure the call centre is of a size that your business will matter to them.

Make sure they record all the calls and keep a log of them. You should have access to call logs and recordings.

Ensure you approve any scripts and define how much flexibility you want. Make sure the callers can speak your language naturally and with minimal accent.

Selection Criteria

o Go for an established call centre that is of the right size so your contract will be something they care about.

o Ensure they record all calls and give you access to the call logs and recordings.

Assessment

o Have them conduct several mock calls with your staff, family and friends.

Metrics

o 90%+ of customer queries resolved during the call.

o Feedback rating of 8-10 for the call centre support staff member.

o Do random surveys of people who phoned in to see how they felt about the call and the way it was handled.

66. Client Satisfaction Surveys

Result

Get honest feedback about the level of service you are providing to your customers to determine if you are creating nett promoters.

Summary

Nett promoters are customers who will rave about your business and recommend you to colleagues and friends. It is a very simple test: ask, "On a scale of 1 to 10, how likely are you to recommend this business to a friend, with 10 meaning you will definitely be recommending this business?"

People who score you an 8 or higher are nett promoters, 6-7 are neutral and 5 or lower are nett detractors, who will complain about your business.

Knowing how your customers rate you and why is essential to improving the all-important Customer Experience.

Ask a few follow-up questions to establish why they gave the score they did.

Keep it to 5 or fewer questions. Let the customer know this at the start of the call so that they are more likely to take the 2 minutes to give feedback.

If your customers tell your callers, "Now is not a good

time", book a time to call them back – then stick to it. If they don't answer, let it go. You can ruin your customer experience with nuisance phone calls too.

With such a simple script and process, this is an obvious choice to outsource.

Make sure your remote staff are empowered to book follow-up appointments if customers request that.

Selection Criteria

- o Excellent spoken language skills.
- o Ability to work during your normal business hours; pick staff in a time zone that is +/- 4hours of yours.
- o Ability to record calls and provide reports on responses.

Assessment

- o Have them conduct mock customer surveys on your staff.

Metrics

- o Set numbers of calls are completed, phone logs and recordings provided.
- o Reports of results are collated clearly with raw data also provided.

67. Customer Relationship Management

Result

Have your CRM current, organised and accessible. Ensure follow-ups and client 'touches' happen as scheduled.

Summary

Customer Relationship Management has become a key part of retaining clients and increasing the 'sale per client' figure. Given it is significantly cheaper to sell to an existing client than to find a new one, this just makes good business sense.

Of course, it takes time to enter all a client's details in a CRM and then to update it regularly. If you have an outsourced CRM manager, this becomes much easier.

Every time you get an email from a new potential client, forward it to your CRM manager. They can create a new client card based off the email sign off.

Every time you have a call or meeting with a client, jot down notes on a scrap of paper with the client's name at the top. Photograph the notes with your phone and email them to your CRM manager to update the customer's details.

Using phone bills and email records, your CRM can capture all the contacts made to each client, without having to pester your local staff to log every activity in your CRM.

All your clients should be 'touched' by you in some way at a regular interval. My preference is for every six weeks if they are not in an active buying cycle.

You can mix this up between emails, phones calls, letters and promotional gifts. Scheduling these and organising them can be done by your CRM manager. Even the letters and mail labels can be put into a mail merge ready for printing and sending by local staff.

Selection Criteria

- o Familiar with your CRM platform. Alternatively, can recommend and train you on one if you do not already have a chosen CRM platform in place.
- o Able to extract and enter data.
- o Can read your handwriting.

Metrics

- o All client details extracted and entered into cards.
- o All phone bills and email records searched to ensure all client contact logs are up-to-date.
- o All regular client 'touches' are scheduled and managed.

Books

68. Book Editing

Result

Improvement in flow of book and overall writing quality, refines and clears any ambiguity in conveying the message of the book. Can also be used for other written materials: manuscripts, letters, marketing materials, web posts, emails, video scripts, etc.

Summary

Hiring an editor can raise the standard for quality of your work. Though an editor cannot turn a mediocre work into a masterpiece, an editor can make a good work better.

Provide the complete manuscript to the editor, along with a synopsis for better understanding of the purpose of the book. In case of a foreign language, provide a sample translation with the manuscript and synopsis.

Inform the editor of the type of editing you need:

- o Line editing, which includes the entire gamut of editing, from conceptualisation to line-by-line
- o Developmental/structural editing, which involves editing the structure of the book to ensure the whole book fit together in a sequential and logical manner.
- o Copyediting, where the editor can only make grammatical changes, catch repetitions in words and phrases, watch out for syntax errors, etc.

Lead the editor through the manuscript once. Answer any questions the editor may have regarding your work to ensure timely transformation of your manuscript into a typescript.

Selection Criteria

- o Know your requirements. Do you need someone who has knowledge of different manual styles, generally only necessary for academic or legal writing, do you want a creative editor, or someone who could just copyedit?

- o Look at the editor's credentials, the types of books they have worked on, and the feedback from their clients.

Assessment

- o Video interview. You must like them and want to work with them. A book is very personal, you have to have trust.

- o Ask them to edit 1,000 words of your manuscript.

Metrics

- o A flawless, better-organised and more engaging manuscript.
- o Adds knowledge to your writing skills.
- o Your work looks brilliant to you and to readers

69. Ghost Writing

Result

Have a book written for you and published as your work.

Summary

A book gives you credibility in your field. People who used to ask, "Why should I listen to you and buy from you?" now just accept you as an authority on your subject.

The ability to outsource to a competent writer to do the heavy lifting of writing a book has made it far easier to become a published author. The advent of self-publishing and print-on-demand services has meant that you can get a book in print extremely cheaply and don't have to do large print runs to have your book available for purchase.

Once you know the topic of your book, post a job looking for suitable ghost writers.

Break your project into milestones so that you have control and input at each step of the process:

- o Book mind-mapped and outlined.
- o Chapter layout and summary to show flow and content of book.
- o Introduction submitted.
- o First 3 chapters submitted.

- 50% of book completed.
- 100% of book completed.
- All changes incorporated.

Ensure you have a condition that all rights and attribution to the material will belong to you and that they will not have the right to publish it or attribute their name to it.

Selection Criteria

- Excellent creative or professional writing skills.
- Work history of lengthy writing tasks with top feedback.
- Read samples of their work. Is it engaging and well-written? Do you want to read more? Would you be happy putting your name to this?

Metrics

- All content is relevant and engaging.
- Book passes online plagiarism check to ensure it hasn't been copied and pasted from somewhere else.
- Each milestone is submitted by deadline.

70. Biography Writing

Result

Get your life story in print, told the way you want it told.

Summary

Find a ghost writer who is willing to spend the time getting to know you. They will have to have an in-depth understanding of who you are in order to get a good result.

Make a start yourself before you select a writer. Take notes of your achievements, write a timeline of your life and place every achievement on it.

Grab a ruled notepad and devote one page to each year of your life. Record everything you can remember. Have your family and friends do the same.

Once you have this level of detail, select your writer. Have them conduct several phone interviews with you over a couple of weeks to learn more.

Once they have a better understanding, they may want to interview important people in your life to get more of a picture on events.

Break the project into milestones and have them submit a book overview and chapter layout, then each chapter as they complete it.

Remember, this is not an autobiography, so it only has to

contain the facts the writer can research and ascertain. It doesn't need to include everything that ever happened in your life. This way you can control what is omitted, what is glossed over and what is given pride of place.

Selection Criteria

- o Excellent creative or professional writing skills.
- o Work history of lengthy writing tasks with top feedback.
- o Read samples of their work. Is it engaging and well-written? Do you want to read more? Would you be happy if this was written about you?

Metrics

- o All content is relevant and engaging.
- o Book passes online plagiarism check to ensure it hasn't been copied and pasted from somewhere else.
- o Each milestone is submitted by deadline.
- o The book is an accurate representation of your life.

71. Book Typesetting and Layout

Result

A book that is well set out, easy to read and navigate, ready for printing and publishing as an eBook.

Summary

There is quite an art to creating a book that is easy to read and feels right. We take it for granted, as most publishers employ highly-paid, full-time professional formatters whose career is getting this right.

If you are going to self-publish and use a print-on-demand service, you might find out how wrong a poorly-formatted book can feel to read, unless you engage a formatter and layout specialist.

Thankfully, this is fairly cheap to do. You could teach yourself from the internet if you had a few weeks to spare. Fortunately, many people do.

Pick the book size you want to use – visit your bookshelf or library to see how they feel. Look at different fonts. There are some simple tools you can download that will tell you what font is used on any book or webpage.

Decide if you want chapter titles at the top of each page and where you want the page numbers. The clearer you are, the better the result will feel.

The formatter will worry about indexes, title fonts and

insets, how much margin to leave around each page and where to position the text.

You should end up with a print book and eBook that feel comfortable to read. In other words, you don't notice the format, you just read. After all, you have been reading for years, you will only notice if something is wrong.

Selection Criteria

- o Completed multiple projects with excellent feedback.
- o Familiar with software that is used by your chosen platform or press.
- o Able to produce a finished eBook with index and menu functionality, where required.

Metrics

- o Book completed and ready to print.
- o eBook complete and ready for people to download and read.

72. Book Cover Design

Result

An eye-catching cover design that epitomises your book. Title and tag line are clear and well-integrated in the design.

Summary

Most people judge a book by its cover. It is the first aspect of your book a customer will see, so it has to engage their attention.

There are so many books in print and it is easy to purchase them and have them delivered. People want great content, but if the cover doesn't grab them, they won't pause to look further.

If you haven't invested time and effort into a great cover, it will appear that you probably haven't invested time and effort into great content either. Simple, logical.

Unless you want to pay for it, a cover design artist isn't going to read your book. So you will need to prepare a synopsis for them.

It is up to you to choose the title and tag line. This is as important as the cover art.

Make sure you negotiate unlimited changes to the design so you can keep tweaking it until it is perfect.

The more of an idea you can give your designer, the less

time it is likely to take to get it right.

Selection Criteria

- o Excellent design credentials, preferably a Bachelor's in Graphic Design.
- o You like their samples of design work and art work.
- o They are able to communicate effectively and understand detailed descriptions of what you want and expect.
- o You receive the cover in a range of files to cover all your publishing needs: pdf, jpeg are the key ones. You will need one in each format with your name, title and tag line and the same files with no name, title, etc.

Metrics

- o Several sketches and rough designs submitted for you to give feedback on.
- o Your chosen design developed in line with your input and requests.
- o A cover design that you love. Keep on requesting changes until you do. This matters!
- o If the project is a bit off-track, don't be afraid to go back to the drawing board.

73. Illustration

Result

Well-designed, enchanting illustrations completed for you book or publication.

Summary

A picture says a thousand words.

Given that, the pictures you use in your book have a much bigger impact than several pages of written content. Anyone who flicks through the pages will stop at the illustrations to get an idea of your book.

You will need to be explicit in your requirements and expectations. Make sure you know what you want, otherwise how can anyone give it to you?

If you are not sure what you want, get Googling. Start looking at all sorts of illustration types and styles and see what you like.

Make sure you like the style of illustration that the remote artist has in their portfolio.

Also make sure that they will rescind all rights to the work, although you may choose to attribute the work to them.

Remember, you are dealing with an artist. You need to give them room to work and express themselves. Too tight a control, and you are likely to stifle them and detrimentally effect the art they produce.

If you are worried, have them submit one illustration at a time. Then provide helpful, specific feedback.

Be gentle with these fragile and idealistic souls. You need them right now.

Selection Criteria

- o   You like their portfolio of work.
- o   You can communicate effectively with them to describe what you need.

Metrics

- o   Illustrations completed to your requirements.
- o   Illustrations match the style of their portfolio.
- o   Art delivered by the deadline.

74. Still Life Paintings from Photographs

Result

Get artwork that incorporates real people and places.

Summary

Ever wanted to read your child a picture-book where they were the star? With not just their name, but their likeness in the book.

Do you want to have a Directors' Hall of Fame with portraits of the company Founders and Directors? Even just an amazing gift for someone?

Find an artist who is talented in the medium you require. Give them a selection of photographs of your subject, and explain the setting you want.

If it is a painting, the artist will likely do sketches first. Request that these are sent through for your input.

If the design is for a book, you will just need an HD image of the painting.

If you want to hang it on your wall, you will need the original canvas. Make sure the canvas and paints used will be able to pass successfully through your immigration controls without huge cost (canvas and most paints are fine – it is generally plant and animal products that are the problem).

Once the artist has finished the painting, have them

remove it from the frame and send you the rolled canvas. You can even pay shipping on arrival.

Be prepared for the re-stretching of the canvas onto a frame locally to cost 30 times what you paid for the artwork!

Selection Criteria

- o You like the style of the paintings in their portfolio.

Metrics

- o Artwork complete to your specifications.
- o Is it a true-life representation of the subject?
- o Is 100% in-proportion with the photos?

75. Translation

Result

Your book or text translated into another language in a way that still makes it interesting and engaging, whilst at the same time, broadening your potential market reach.

Summary

Google can translate text for you if you just want to understand it. It is a different task to translate meaning in a way that is gripping and interesting to read, and grammatically correct.

Awarding this is a difficult decision to make. How will you know if it has been done well? How do you know the outsourced translator isn't just using Google to translate?

Trust but verify. Find where the local community for that ethnicity is located in your nearest large city. All communities that share a common language tend to congregate together. Go down and put an ad on the community notice-board. You will give them your book for free if they give you feedback on it.

Alternatively, you can engage outsourced readers fluent in the language you are translating into.

Have them score the text of the book on a scale of 1-10 for:

    o   Readability and flow of text.

- o Use of correct grammar and sentence structure.
- o Use of colloquial language.
- o Interest of the content - this is more for your benefit than the translator.

Selection Criteria

- o They claim to be fluent in both languages. Ideally, select a native speaker of the language you are translating into.
- o Good work history feedback for translation projects.

Metrics

- o Translated text scores an 8-10 with your sample readers for:
  - - Readability and flow of text.
  - - Use of correct grammar and sentence structure.
  - - Use of colloquial language.

Accounting and Bookkeeping

76. Entering Receipts

Result

Have the receipts for all your purchases entered every week so your bookkeeping is always up-to-date.

Summary

Having a shoe-box full of receipts to enter all at once two days before the deadline is no fun. Usually we resort to paying a local bookkeeper or accountant to enter these, or try and avoid that cost by wasting days of our precious time doing it ourselves.

Hire yourself an offshore accountant who can do this for you at a minimal cost.

Every time you make a purchase, take a photo of the receipt. You can download a photo app that automatically syncs to your cloud storage when you are in a Wi-Fi zone, so you just snap and forget.

You can still keep the receipts for your paper records if you are old-school but remember, receipts often fade, photos don't. Plus, the photo is now stored on your phone and in the cloud, far less likely to get lost than that flimsy receipt, and already in date order.

Give your remote accountant a link or read-only access to the folder that the photos get uploaded to. That way you can have confidence no files are accidentally deleted.

If you have a cloud-based accounting package, your remote accountant will enter your receipts into that directly for you.

If you just want the data to give to your local accountant to do your tax returns, simply have the receipts entered into a spreadsheet with the file-names of the photos.

Selection Criteria

- o Qualified accountant or similar qualification, e.g. Bachelor of Commerce.
- o Competent with your cloud accounting package or Microsoft Excel.

Assessment

- o Most software has a 'test company' setup, or you can register for a 30-day free trial with a mock company. Do this and have your remote accountant enter 15-20 sample receipts.

Metrics

- o All receipts are entered 100% accurately and in the correct accounts.
- o All data entered at least weekly, and you are notified when complete.
- o Negotiate a rate per 100 receipts. You can pay per receipt, but will pay less by the hundred as you sound like you will be providing a lot of work.

77. Enter Bills and Invoices Payable

Result

Have all your accounts payable up-to-date so you can manage cash flow more effectively and pay bills when you need to.

Summary

Receiving bills is never fun. It is enough work just to pay them, yet alone entering them into your accounting software so you can schedule payment and organise cash flow and current reports.

When the bills and account invoices come in, place them to one side, in a tray, not the bin!

Once a week, scan them all. You can buy a cheap multifunction printer with an automatic document feeder that will scan them all at the push of a button. Or it may be easier to photograph them with your phone and have them uploaded to the cloud directly. Again the advantage here is they can be easily ordered according to date.

Your remote accountant can then enter them into your cloud-based accounting software.

You can log on at any time and see what bills are due for payment, and what is coming up over the next few weeks for payment.

If you have regular bills, like phone bills, rent, car registration or insurance, you can have your remote accountant set up a repeating invoice so that you can see those bills coming ahead of time.

Selection Criteria

- o Qualified accountant or similar qualification, e.g. Bachelor of Commerce.
- o Competent with your cloud accounting package.

Assessment

- o Most software has a 'test company' setup, or you can register for a 30-day free trial with a mock company. Have your remote accountant enter 5 invoices and run an Aged Payables report for you.

Metrics

- o All bills and invoices are entered 100% accurately and in the correct accounts.
- o All data entered at least weekly, and you are notified when complete.
- o Negotiate a rate per 100 invoices. You can pay per bill, but will pay less by the hundred as you sound like you will be providing a lot of work.

78. Invoicing and Follow-up

Result

Have your clients invoiced regularly to ensure good cash flow. Have the horrible task of chasing payment done on a systemised schedule to reduce late payments.

Summary

It should be the 'fun' part of accounting - organising for money to come in. It's still accounting, though.

If you can organise to have your invoices done and sent for you, it makes life that much more fun.

How you organise this will depend on your business and how you invoice. There are plenty of options to communicate with your remote accountant: timesheets, emails, send the quote and tell them when each item is complete, or upload voice memos telling them what you need invoiced.

Make sure you are copied into the emails going out with the invoices attached, just to verify.

The really wonderful part is that you can have your remote accountant follow up to make sure you get paid when you should, or at least, sooner.

Have your remote accountant draft a series of polite emails following up on payment, the first to go out a few days before payment is due just to check that all required information was sent.

You can also have them follow up with polite phone calls. Remember the old adage, the squeaky wheel gets the oil – or in this case, gets paid!

It doesn't have to be obnoxious or painful, just consistent, professional reminders that you are owed money. Plus, the great benefit is you never have to get stressed or frustrated by slow playing clients.

Selection Criteria

- o Qualified accountant or similar qualification, e.g. Bachelor of Commerce.
- o Competent with your cloud accounting package.
- o Able to speak professionally and courteously so they can make follow up phone calls.

Assessment

- o Have them submit a sample follow-up email addressed to a fictitious client, requesting payment for an overdue debt.

Metrics

- o All invoices and payments are entered 100% accurately and in the correct accounts.
- o All follow-up happens as scheduled. Write a plan, 2 days before, 1 day after, 1 week after, then every day the following week, etc.

Result

Have all your bank transactions reconciled weekly and any unknown payments flagged and reported on. Avoid bogus charges and fraud on your account.

Summary

Identity theft is becoming a huge issue. The smartest thieves don't just drain your account, but make ongoing small withdrawals or purchases. How often do you go over your statement and reconcile payments?

If you issue company debit cards to your staff, you can also monitor spending patterns and unusual transactions.

If you have your receipts, bills and invoices entered, it is then so simple to have your account reconciled as well.

Have your remote accountant reconcile all your accounts at least weekly and send you a Reconciliation Report showing any irreconcilable transactions. You can follow up on these straightaway.

If the transactions were made by your staff, you can track this as their card number is partially on the transaction record. Have your remote accountant follow up directly with them and report back to you.

Selection Criteria

- Qualified accountant or similar qualification, e.g. Bachelor of Commerce.
- Competent with your cloud accounting package.

Metrics

- All accounts are reconciled weekly.
- You receive a Reconciliation Report weekly.

80. Financial Reports

Result

Have all your company's key lead and lag reports prepared for you weekly/fortnightly. Have a dashboard of key financial indicators submitted weekly to monitor your performance at a glance.

Summary

Knowing your numbers is a key requirement for any business. Not knowing the numbers is a primary reason for failure amongst small businesses.

One remote accountant can do all the tasks on the previous pages. You can have them booked for one day a week and have them complete this reporting once all the basic tasks are done. You will likely get them for a twentieth the cost of local bookkeeper, so use them!

Have your key reports sent through P&L, Cashflow, Balance Sheet, Debtors Report and Aged Payables.

That's great, but you probably won't look at it all as thoroughly as you should. So develop the 5-6 key financial metrics for your business. You can change them later if necessary.

The key metrics you choose will vary widely, depending on the business and industry you are in. You are looking for the key indicators that things are going well. If you could change just 5 numbers to make your business amazing, what would they be?

Whatever you pick, set what the numbers look like when they are great (green), acceptable (yellow), and bad (red).

Have these key metrics sent through on a single piece of paper or screen. Make sure each number is highlighted in the appropriate colour.

Now you can see at a glance what is under control, what needs work and what needs your urgent attention. Now you can delve into the reports, just focusing on the critical areas.

Selection Criteria
- o Qualified accountant or similar qualification, e.g. Bachelor of Commerce.
- o Competent with your cloud accounting package.

Assessment
- o Have them suggest what they feel would be the key dashboard metrics for your business.
- o Submit a sample dashboard report showing the layout they would use.

Metrics
- o Dashboard comes in every week/fortnight on the designated day.
- o All reports come through weekly/fortnightly.

81. Financial Analytics

Result

Have an in-depth financial analysis of your company's performance completed to help you make those bid decisions.

Summary

Should you keep a department running, hire or fire staff, purchase that equipment? Do you need to extend your bank loan? Are you in a good position to ask for funding or investment?

These are big decisions. To make good decisions, you need good information.

How is your company performing? Is it profitable, solvent, liquid and stable? How do its performance ratios compare to other businesses in your industry? Will your creditors or investors be happy with the numbers you are submitting?

Better find out!

Get a senior accountant to go over all the figures that your remote accountant has so carefully collated.

This should be someone other than your day-to-day remote accountant.

Find someone with a Master's in Finance who can take your numbers and pull them apart.

Make sure you get a full report, with suggestions made in plain language, not confusing or dense financial jargon. It should suggest areas of improvement and address any specific questions you have.

Selection Criteria

- o Master's in Finance or similar advanced qualification.
- o Competent with your cloud accounting package.
- o History of auditing financial analysis.
- o Good spoken language skills, so they can talk you through the report.
- o If you are making a big decision, select 2 candidates as a double redundancy. You don't want to base your decision on a report where someone accidentally added a zero to a column.

Metrics

- o Comprehensive report written in plain language.
- o Answers your questions succinctly.
- o Shows any areas for concern.
- o Is verified as accurate by a second report, or audit cross check.

82. Budgeting and Forecasting

Result

Have your annual company budget completed with 'what-if' analyses built in so that you can project different scenarios.

Summary

Budgeting and planning is an essential business tool. It gives you something to aim for and measure your performance against.

If you have been trading for at least a year, you can outsource this task very easily.

Have your remote accountant create an annual budget based on your historical performance. If you have been trading for a few years, they can project forward based on how you have been trending.

Once they have this in basic format, they book a call with you so you can go over each area for an hour or two. Let them guide you through each line item and just answer what your gut feel tells you: "Yes, we will hire more staff, a receptionist and a personal assistant for me!" or "No, insurance will stay the same." Or maybe, "Yes, we will need to buy new computers for the new staff."

Make sure the document notes with your assumptions.

Once the budget is looking good, the remote accountant

needs to factor in 'what-if' analyses.

Doing a 'what-if' analysis lets you see what would happen if your sales increased by 30%. What would your costs do? What if your sales dropped by 30% and certain line costs went up? Would you still be profitable?

This lets you quickly prepare 3 budgets: optimistic, realistic and pessimistic. How does the company look under each possible scenario? Do you need contingency plans for rapid growth or downsizing?

Once you finalise your budget, have it imported into your accounting package to track your performance against.

Selection Criteria

- o Qualified accountant or similar qualification, e.g. Bachelor of Commerce.
- o Competent with your cloud accounting package.
- o Can use a budgeting platform that you are familiar with or can learn quickly.
- o Can understand and manipulate data and trends.

Metrics

- o Annual budget completed, accurate and understandable.
- o Incorporates your forecasts and assumptions.
- o Has easy-to-use and understand 'what-if' functionality.

83. Spreadsheet Creation and Maintenance

Result

Have complex spreadsheets designed for tasks that don't fit inside your accounting packages. Ongoing support and troubleshooting.

Summary

No matter what your business, there always seem to be some figures you want to see in a particular way that your accounting package just can't handle. Maybe you need to generate a specific progress report for a department or team, or track performance and likely bonus costs.

Most of us end up resorting to a good old spreadsheet. They are a powerful tool, but can get amazingly complex very quickly. Plus, they forever seem to be having issues.

If you are better at using spreadsheets than programing formulas and complex operations, have someone do it for you.

Give them your requirements: what you need to measure or track and how you want it to look. What information do you want to see? Do you want a dashboard with visual images showing performance?

Have them make all required changes until it is working for you, but remember, it will never be perfect!

Then negotiate a fixed 'maintenance contract'. That is an agreed annual fee to fix any issues that pop up or minor changes you need made.

Doing a fixed fee provides incentive to get the spreadsheet as bug-free as possible. An hourly maintenance rate encourages bugs that need time spent to fix them.

Selection Criteria

o First-rate skills with your spreadsheet of choice. Pick someone who has completed the test for this software through the outsourcing platform. They should rank in the top 25%.

Metrics

o A clean, easy-to-use spreadsheet with all required functionality.
o Staff can learn to use the spreadsheet quickly and with accuracy, ie user-friendly.
o Not needing maintenance or troubleshooting more than once every couple of months.

84. Auditing

Result

Conduct a full internal audit.

Summary

Having an internal audit helps ensure the integrity of your information, protects against fraud and helps you comply with local laws.

This is a complex task and often involves specialists across several areas, such as accounting, IT and HR.

For this reason it is usually better to engage an agency or team who special in company audits. Look for teams with extensive experience with local companies and at least some experience in your industry.

This is likely to need a reasonable amount of local support as the auditors request further information and data. Task an admin person to provide what is requested. If they are unable to provide what is needed, then they can come to you.

Don't give this task to your most trusted staff member. It may even be worth getting in a temp. Only the staff you trust are ever in a position to perpetrate fraud.

Audits are never fun. At least this way you can keep the cost down.

Selection Criteria

- o An agency or team who has experience auditing companies in your country.
- o Some experience with local companies in your industry.
- o Team contains all skillsets relevant to your business.

Metrics

- o A full report detailing risks and risk management within your company.
- o Report on core areas of financial and IT control.
- o Report on supply-chain analysis and recommendations.
- o May provide reports on culture and ethics within your company.

85. Financial Prospectus Writing

Result

Have a well-crafted, accurate and engaging company prospectus prepared for potential investors.

Summary

Raising capital is exciting and nerve-racking. You want to do everything you can to present the best, most complete picture of your company.

Using external experts just makes sense. Of course, paying them will reduce how good your figures look!

This is another great place for a coordinated effort. Have your accountant and financial analyst prepare the data and write the reports.

Next engage a content writer with a financial background to prepare the reports and data in an engaging way that doesn't put the reader to sleep, whilst maintaining the financial integrity of the data.

Then you will need to engage a graphic designer to put all the content, tables and graphs into a masterpiece that you want to hand out to your friends.

Use the guidelines already discussed for 'content writers'; just add a criteria that they have a solid financial background. Also use the guidelines for 'graphic designers' in the marketing chapter.

The graphic designer is the perfect person to appoint as Project Manager. This solves the issue of you being the hub of the wheel that all communication has to go through. They are best placed to request the data, graphs and content are presented in particular formats, you don't want them preparing graphs or changing table layouts themselves!

Selection Criteria

- o The content writer must have a solid understanding of financial principles.
- o The graphic designer should have significant report-generating experience. They will also need excellent communication skills if you are going to appoint them as project manager.

Metrics

- o A well-presented prospectus that accurately outlines your company in a fascinating way that will make you proud. This is important! Insist on as many changes as you need until they get it right.

86. Business Intelligence and Data Mining

Result

Find useful and meaningful patterns and information in large amounts of business and market data.

Summary

Data mining is aimed at taking large amounts of raw information, and extracting said information in such a way that it is understandable and useful for decision-making.

Finding patterns to predict future behaviour based on previous performance is always dangerous, but it beats wild guesswork.

Using wider market data, you can search for business opportunities and ways to more effectively implement management strategy. The aim is to take advantage of market conditions.

This data is available to the public, so how do you sort it to find what you want? Start by understanding your capabilities and opportunities as a business. In order to act on these opportunities, what would you need or want to see happen? What assumptions would you need to make?

Now engage a remote data miner to see if those conditions exist, or are likely to exist in the future.

If you are using data that you have collected as a company, identify what changes, savings or expansions you would like to make. Have the data tested to see if it supports making this move.

Remember, you need good data to get good information. You need good information to make good decisions.

Selection Criteria

- o High-level mathematical qualifications, Bachelors or Masters.
- o Secondary qualification in business, an MBA is ideal.
- o Proposal includes a clear plan as to how they intend to data mine the raw information to look for patterns.

Metrics

- o Complete and accurate report and conclusion.
- o Areas covered are relevant and meet original job description.
- o Figures and conclusions can be verified from the raw data.
- o Project delivered on time.

Web Design and Optimisation

87. Webpage Design

Result

A website with full design and functionality including home page, landing pages, full menu and email opt-in with auto responder.

Summary

Having bought your domain name, you need a website. There are plenty of places you can buy a cheap brochure page, so why get one personally designed?

- o Your design is personal.
- o Unlimited changes.
- o Ongoing team at low rates to update, add content and pages, develop and grow the site as you grow.

You will need to get your own content - see separate page for outsourcing that. This remote staff member is usually a team or company in a country with significantly lower cost of living, so you can hire a full team with all specialities for a fraction of engaging a local web development team.

If you don't have the energy to design what you want from scratch, you can modify another. In posting your ad, be specific that you want to modify one of the designers' previous sites, which they own the IP for. Ask for a list of sites they have that meet this criteria, find the site you like and you have found your team! Then just agree to

236

unlimited changes until it fits what you want.

Selection Criteria

They must know what they are doing, so check out their previous projects. Were they good to work with on these projects? Check their feedback ratings.

- o Previous projects at the level and complexity you are planning for your website.
- o Feedback scores from previous projects.
- o Reasonable hourly rate to hire for future website updates and modification.

Metrics

This is a fixed price project, with a cost for ongoing hourly rate work when you want the site content, look or functionality updated – so make sure you are provided with both costs.

- o Fixed price with agreed milestones, ie home page, menu system, other pages, content inserted, etc.
- o Do not release a milestone payment until you are happy with content.
- o Final payment when website is live.

88. Integrate Web Tools into your Site

Result

A website with most current functionality and tools to drive leads and sales.

Summary

If you already have a web page, does it look dated? Does it have the most up-to-date tools integrated into it in order to drive leads and sales?

How many places on your landing page do you have for capturing emails for potential clients? Do you have calls to action? Are page visitors able to download an eBook, articles, templates or useful data in return for giving up their email address?

You need to make sure the second they enter their email address, the promised goodie is delivered to their email account. No one likes waiting.

Do you have somewhere for customers to purchase directly from your website? Do you redirect them to somewhere they can purchase?

Can you monitor who visits your site and from where. Do you know what pages they look at on your site and how long they spend there?

Getting all this is not complex. Create an outsourced project to optimize your website and make a list of the minimum functionality you want to include.

Have remote web optimizers bid on your project and make recommendations and suggestions as to what they can incorporate and at what cost. Bang – your website is looking current and driving your business again!

Selection Criteria

- o Incorporates all the functionality tools you specified.
- o Has completed similar projects that look good and run smoothly; check their work history.
- o Offers additional functionality that you now definitely want!

Metrics

- o Your website incorporates the modern tools and functionality that you requested.
- o Your page still loads quickly with the new scripts. Use Google's page analytics tools, insist on a minimum score of 85/100 for desktop and mobile and all "should fix" issues addressed.

89. Your Website Made Mobile Friendly

Result

Have your existing website transitioned to a mobile page that allows premium viewing on mobile devices.

Summary

Mobile devices have surpassed desktop devices as the preferred way to access the internet and view webpages. If your page is not mobile friendly, you are losing the majority of your potential views.

If you are happy with your desktop website and content, but it is not mobile friendly, you need a mobile version of your website designed.

This will not change the way your website appears on a desktop computer, it will simply create a separate mobile webpage.

Go through and prioritise what you want viewers to see. They will be looking at it on a much smaller screen, so you have to decide what is going to come up.

Take some time to remember why you have a website. What purpose do you hope it will serve? Once you are clear about this, you are in a better place to decide what you show people who view your mobile page.

You may also need to pare down or simplify your menu. 3-4 menu tabs is usually the most you want to see on a mobile device. Forget the 'Contact' and 'About' pages, they will scroll down and find those on the bottom menu if they want them. Everyone knows it is standard protocol to have them appear there.

Selection Criteria

- o Check out their work history on your mobile or tablet:
    - Do you like the pages?
    - Are they easy to access and navigate from your mobile device?
    - Is it clear with crisp graphics?
    - Does it load quickly?
    - Are they versatile? Do they have many different types of projects completed, or do they always copy the same style?

Metrics

- o Your mobile webpage has the desired information displayed in a user friendly way.
- o The design is in keeping with your brand.
- o Can viewers still contact you and buy from you?
- o Your mobile page loads quickly. Use Google's page analytics tools, insist on a minimum score of 85/100 for your mobile page and all "should fix" issues addressed.

Result

Your website is easy to navigate and find information on. Your subpages have optimised metatag keywords.

Summary

A user friendly website experience is essential. Most first impressions with yourself or your business will now be made on the web. So your customer experience here is as important as any physical location you have, the clothes you wear or the car you drive.

People will judge you on this.

So if people can't find what they want quickly and easily on your site, they will leave.

Apple took off because Steve Jobs demanded that he be able to navigate to any song on the iPod in 3 clicks or fewer. How many clicks does it take to find something on your page?

A bit of time spent strategizing the layout of your menu system, the site map or menu tree, can help you see how things are laid out and what improvements you could make.

Having plenty of internal page hyperlinks also helps people jump around when they need to.

Your metatags are the keywords that help search

engines land people on the right page when they click through. Spend some time simplifying and deciding on the best words or phrase to describe that page.

If people navigate directly to a page from a search engine, what will that page do for their first impression?

Selection Criteria

- o An SEO expert or web design strategist.
- o Ability to help you brainstorm and clarify your purpose for having a webpage.
- o Able to implement changes to optimise website experience.

Assessment

- o Provide a link to your site. Ask applicants to list the top 3 things they would change. This is useful as it not only helps you select candidates, it also offers you more ideas to implement.

Metrics

- o Your webpage experience feels intuitive and user-friendly.
- o An acquaintance, or anyone not familiar with your website, can locate information you suggest within 3 clicks.

91. Database Design for your Website

Result

A database-driven website that is dynamic and responsive. A database that you can manage and edit.

Summary

Almost all dynamic webpages are database driven. A dynamic webpage is responsive and allows information to change every time the page is loaded, based on what a user does.

Databases are essential for web stores and can be very useful for capturing, storing and utilising customer data. The main benefit, however, is an awesome webpage that feels cutting-edge, because it is dynamic and responsive.

Start by brainstorming what you want your site to do. What do you want it to respond to? What data do you want to update regularly? What do you want to update depending on where the page viewer arrives from and how they behave?

This will help you identify what you need to store on the database. Keep it broad at first, as you can assign specific fields later. What do you need the website to do? What data does it need to display or capture?

Once you are clear on what you need, you can get your remote database designer to start modelling and mapping it. They will most likely create a Relational Database and interrelate all the cells and information to each other in an organised way.

At this point, you should bow out. The language will get complex and involved. You are best to stay at a high level and know what you want it to do, rather than getting bogged down in the technical jargon.

The goal of a good database is to be efficient, easy to access and have the ability to be scaled. Be ready for the fact that this may involve ongoing maintenance and costs. You can negotiate a fixed annual maintenance and upgrading fee into the original contract.

Selection Criteria

- o Experience in design and administration of web databases.
- o Ensure they are familiar with a database that is used by your website hosting server.

Metrics

- o A fully dynamic, responsive website that maximises user experience.
- o All data stored in a logical, accessible manner that you can retrieve and change without needing to learn to be a professional database administrator.

Result

Have your website list as high as possible in the organic rankings on Google and other search engines.

Summary

33% of people click on the top organic result in Google when they search for something. This more than halves, dropping to 16% for the second place and declines into single digits beyond 3rd place. If you aren't on the first page of results, you get less than 1% of the clicks!

So, you need to get noticed by Google.

There is an entire industry built around this and trying to cheat Google. Google has some of the best minds in the world working to keep one step ahead.

It is a dark art and a tricky area. Every time someone finds a loophole to exploit Google and get organic listings higher, they sell it and business goes crazy.

The problem is, every time Google finds the loophole, they not only close it, but punish those who they feel cheated the system.

So with SEO, cheapest isn't always best.

If you are looking for a quick fix, it is almost always an attempt to cheat.

Expect to end up with an SEO strategy that is

multifaceted and involves you pulling together a team of outsourced staff for various roles.

An SEO implementation plan with key tasks, dates and individuals responsible for completing each task has the best chance of showing consistent, long-term effects.

You may consider hiring an agency or team who can do this for you, or your SEO manager may offer to project manage the process for you. Someone needs to drive the process and keep people accountable.

Selection Criteria

- o Look for proposals that offer:
    - A structured approach.
    - Long and short term goals.
    - Ongoing support.
    - Multi-faceted approach.

Metrics

- o You rank #1 (or in the top 3) in the organic listings on Google for your chosen keywords

Apps and Software

93. App Development

Result

Have your idea turned into an app that is listed on the app store and makes you rich.

Summary

Got a great idea for an app? Seems I can't get through a party without hearing about 3 or 4 peoples 'amazing app ideas'. Like any idea, it's far more about the execution than the idea.

Outsourcing this just makes sense. There are a few golden rules to follow though:

1) Be very clear on what you are doing and the result you want – communicate this effectively.
Test: Give your description to a friend or colleague. Can they describe exactly what you want without asking further questions?
2) Choose your developer carefully, and make sure they understand your requirements, budget and milestones. Can they really deliver?
3) Have the developer sign a Non-Disclosure Agreement (NDA).
4) Provide prompt feedback and keep in constant communication with your developer.
5) Test several beta versions.
6) Make sure you have staggered the milestones.

Hold back at least 50% of the payment for when the app is approved by the app store.

7) Make sure you get a copy of all your app project files from the developer.

Selection Criteria

o Strong app development history with top feedback scores, never use someone new to any outsourcing platform, regardless of the story they spin you!

o Look at the whole proposal, not just the price.

o Solid communication skills.

o Demonstrates an understanding of the proposal from the limited information you provide on the project post.

o Will they submit your app to the app store?

Metrics

o Each milestone achieved and altered as per your requirements.

o Deadlines adhered to.

o Beta versions match your requirements.

o App accepted by the app store.

Result

Have an app that your staff can download and use to report and monitor progress and drive policy adherence.

Summary

Using paper checklists and spreadsheet reports have serious drawbacks; they are not user-friendly and most staff hate them.

So why not take that policy checklist, progress reporting, logging tool, or operations manual and turn it into a user-friendly app that your staff can always have with them on their phone or tablet?

This is a fairly simple and cost-effective exercise when outsourced.

There is less of an issue with the idea being stolen as well. Some of the same principles still apply:

1) Be very clear about what you are doing and the result you want – communicate this effectively.
2) Choose your developer carefully. Make sure they understand your requirements, budget and milestones. Can they really deliver?
3) Test several beta versions.
4) Make sure you have staggered the milestones. Hold back at least 50% of the payment for when

the app is approved by the app store.

5) Ensure the developer will submit and keep your app on the app store for you.

Selection Criteria

- o Strong app development history with top feedback scores. Never use someone new to any outsourcing platform, regardless of the story they spin you!
- o Look at the whole proposal, not just the price.
- o Solid communication skills.
- o Demonstrates an understanding of the proposal from the full job description you post for pricing and quotes.
- o They submit your app to the app store and keep it there.

Metrics

- o Each milestone achieved and altered as per your requirements.
- o Deadlines adhered to.
- o Beta versions match your requirements.
- o App live on the app store.

95. Software Design

Result

Own the rights to a complete and functional software program.

Summary

Designing software can be a great business. If you get it right. Then all you have to do is sell it. There are few ongoing costs to scale it.

So what do you have to do in order to get your software concept designed and programed?

Firstly, you need to know what you want, how it will look and operate. Create a mind map showing every aspect of the software. Now map out and link the key functions you want it to perform.

You should now have a good idea of the complexity involved in your project. Make sure you hire a development team who have dealt with projects of at least equal complexity previously.

Yes, you are looking for a team. Software development takes multiple skillsets and needs central control and project management. Find a team or company that specialises in this.

Communication is the key to getting a good result. Make sure you like your project team and are able to communicate effectively with them.

Stay actively involved through every step of the process. The more involvement you have, the closer the result will be to your envisioned outcome.

Selection Criteria

- o Have completed several projects of at least equal complexity.
- o Willing to sign all rights over to you.
- o Use modern programing tools and principles.
- o Outstanding communication skills.
- o You are able to test the software they have developed previously and can drive it.
- o You like them!

Metrics

- o Milestones completed on time.
- o Results match your clearly defined criteria at every step of the process.
- o Beta programs perform as advertised.
- o Final program delivered within required timeframe.

96. Beta Quality Assurance Testing

Result

Ensure that your beta software or app is functional and will hold up to 'unskilled' use.

Summary

You understand your software or app and it works perfectly for you. Of course! It was your idea and you drove the development. If there was something that didn't work for you, you had it fixed.

Unfortunately, not everyone thinks as logically and carefully as you do. In fact, the world is populated with idiots. So how do you make sure your project is idiot-proof?

Give it to a group of 'big kids' and see if they can break it.

It's easy to find fault. In fact, it's significantly easier to find fault with others and their work than it is to acknowledge success. The more expert you are in a field, the easier it is to find fault.

So locate a group with expertise in the area you have designed your app or software for and have them try it.

Challenge them to find issues and problems with it.

You may be able to find them locally, or you may have to outsource all over the world. Some will require payment, some can be bought with a promise of the final product for free and some will do it for fun.

Take some time to brainstorm where you might advertise or look for Beta QA testers. Get as creative as you can, it will save you money!

Selection Criteria

- o Interested in the area you have developed your app or software for.
- o Has the time available to give it a good try.
- o Willing and able to effectively communicate the issues they found and how they got them to occur.

Metrics

- o This is difficult. You can't really demand fault quotas, as you may have designed a beautiful and flawless work of art. On the other hand, if it is riddled with bugs, the QA testers will stop looking once they hit their quota.

  Look instead for feedback and communication that shows they have understood the software or app and truly tried to use it to its potential.

Design for Construction and Manufacture

97. Architectural Drafting

Result

Have your office or home designed to your exact requirements, ready to submit to your local authority for approval.

Summary

Have you seen what an architect charges? They are usually holier-than-thou types who don't want their artistic integrity and reputation diminished by an interfering busybody. Just because you have to live/work there and are paying their fee. How dare you have input!

So take them out of the equation. Turn your back-of-the-napkin sketches into a scaled floor plan, elevations and sections.

You have full 'artistic control', don't have to deal with illogical, irrational personality types and save yourself a fortune into the bargain.

Look for a remote architect or draftsperson who has formal qualifications and has designed in your local market before. This will save time with them learning the requirements to get drawings passed by your local government body for approval.

Make sure unlimited changes are included. This should

continue after you are happy with the design, right through until you have approval to start construction.

Selection Criteria

- You can communicate successfully with the design team. They listen and respond to requests you make for changes in the proposal - a good sign that they will listen later.
- They have drafted similar projects for your geographic area and understand the design requirements.
- They have previously designed projects similar to what you want to build.

Metrics

- Each stage of the project is aligned with your ideas and incorporates your changes.
- Keep the majority of payment until you are happy.
- Have an additional 20-30% for changes required by your local government. This process can drag on for some time.
- Ensure deadlines are realistic, then enforce them.

98. Interior Decorating

Result

Have a beautifully designed interior for your home or office.

Summary

A building should feel good inside. Most people won't notice great design, they will just feel good and enjoy being in a building. Everyone notices bad design.

If you are designing a new building, give your remote interior decorator the plans and a clear brief. What you like:

1) What colour schemes.
2) Styles of furniture.
3) Types of materials you like, from floors and walls to curtains and lampshades.
4) The required flow and functionality.

If you want to spruce up an existing building, show them what you have to start with. Turn on every light in the place, then take a video tour with your phone's camera. Take focused still shots on areas you want them to prioritise.

Upload the video and stills along with your project outline and budget.

There are companies that specialise in collecting and

distributing current construction costs for every trade and aspect of construction and design for every geographic location on the planet. So your decorator should be able to cost every part of their proposal to meet your budget, wherever they are located in the world.

Selection Criteria

- o Look at their portfolio of work. Do you love it?
- o Are they able to communicate well in their proposal?
- o Do they listen and incorporate requested changes into your proposal? That is a good sign they will take on board what you want later in the project.

Metrics

- o Project is decorated to your specifications and budget.
- o All designs and plans returned by deadline.
- o All your changes and input are incorporated into the project.

99. Industrial and Product Design

Result

Get your brilliantly-designed and engineered products ready for your manufacturing team.

Summary

To take your fantastic idea and convert it into a product that can be manufactured on a large scale takes some doing. Start by carefully mapping out your product concept and its uses.

As part of the design contract, have the remote designer research the marketplace to see what products exist that are similar. How is yours better? Is there a market for it? How well organised and promoted are your competition?

You are then ready to start the design phase. Make sure you and your designer consider the following:

- o Will the design allow the product to function as required?
- o Will the product be reliable and able to withstand use?
- o Can it be made easier to manufacture?
- o Can the design be changed to make manufacture more cost-effective?
- o What are the environmental and cost considerations for the materials required?
- o What quality standard do you want it to meet?

Once you think it is right, it's time to liaise with your manufacturing team. Get their input and suggestions and include these changes in the design.

Finally, build a prototype and test it. Does it perform as you hoped? Terrific – into production!

Selection Criteria

- o Do you like their previous work?
- o Are they responsive to your enquiries?
- o Research their history and client feedback.
- o Interview them to get a better feel for their approach to your project.

Metrics

- o Design meets your original specifications.
- o All changes and pivots along the way are successful and seamlessly merged into the design.
- o Final product is functional and can be manufactured cost-effectively.
- o Deadlines met.

100. CAD Design

Result

Your design is perfectly created in AutoCAD and modelled in 2D or 3D as required.

Summary

To get the best idea of how your project, product or concept will look and work, it is difficult to improve on Computer-Aided Design (CAD).

AutoCAD can include 2D modelling, 3D modelling, rendering and animation.

You get to see how the finished product or project will look, work and interact.

As well as allowing you to see how your product will look, having your design in AutoCAD gives you almost universal ability to distribute it for costing and feedback.

Having your drawings in CAD lets you:

- o   Edit them any time.
- o   Access them on your mobile device to show clients, team members or investors.
- o   Track and undo changes.
- o   Control what aspects you send or print. To reduce confusion, only show the area you are discussing or having priced.
- o   Change scale.

Selection Criteria

- o Access to full version of AutoCAD.
- o Have they designed in your specific area previously?
- o Make sure they have extensive AutoCAD experience and top level feedback.

Metrics

- o AutoCAD matches the paper design.
- o All changes and modification requests are assimilated into the design.
- o All changes tracked, and originals and all modified designs submitted to you.
- o All deadlines met.

An accomplished entrepreneur and speaker, with a career spanning several industries, Craig D Robinson has used outsourcing in all his businesses to leverage the power of people, without the huge cost.

One of his most notable outsourcing achievements was to generate a 570% increase in quotes for his construction company, whilst saving 11% in the estimating department.

Craig is passionate about wellness and adventure. He has completed several trail ultra-marathons, is a qualified skydiving instructor and an avid adventure racer. He stays focused and balanced by spending 7 days in silent meditation every 2 months.

A Father, volunteer firefighter, philanthropist and owner of multiple businesses, Craig also finds time to volunteer with children who suffer from disability and is the founder of a Social Enterprise to help refugees start and run their own businesses.

Craig also consults with a wide range of companies, specialising in creating and implementing systems to outsource mission critical roles.

To connect with Craig, visit www.craigdrobinson.com